OUTDOOR HOME™

Designing
YOUR OUTDOOR HOME

LANDSCAPE
PLANNING
MADE EASY

CREATIVE
PUBLISHING
international

MINNETONKA, MINNESOTA

Credits

Executive Editor: Bryan Trandem
Associate Creative Director: Tim Himsel
Lead Art Director: Gina Seeling
Managing Editor: Jennifer Caliandro
Project Manager: Michelle Skudlarek
Author: Bryan Trandem
Editors: Jerri Farris, Christian Dick
Technical Production Editors:
  Keith Thompson, Philip Schmidt
Copy Editor: Janice Cauley
Mac Designers: Patricia Goar, Kari Johnston,
  Jonathan Hinz, Jon Simpson,
  Brad Webster
Vice President of Photography & Production:
  Jim Bindas
Studio Services Manager: Marcia Chambers
Photo Services Coordinator: Carol Osterhus
Photographers: Tate Carlson, Jamey Mauk,
  Andrea Rugg, Rebecca Schmitt
Photographer Assistants: Greg Wallace,
  Keven Timian
Cover Photography: Lloyd Flanders
Scene Shop Carpenters: Troy Johnson,
  Dan Widerski
Manager, Production Services: Kim Gerber
Production Manager: Stasia Dorn

Copyright© Creative Publishing
international, Inc.
5900 Green Oak Drive
Minnetonka, MN 55343
1-800-328-3895
All rights reserved
Printed in U.S.A. by R. R. Donnelley & Sons Co.

President: Iain Macfarlane
Group Director, Book Development: Zoe Graul
Director, Creative Development: Lisa Rosenthal
Executive Managing Editor: Elaine Perry

Created by: The Editors of Creative
Publishing international, Inc. in
cooperation with Black & Decker.
BLACK&DECKER is a trademark of the
Black & Decker Corporation and is used
under license.

Library of Congress
Cataloging-in-Publication Data
Designing your outdoor home: landscape
planning made easy.
p.   cm. --(Black & Decker outdoor home)
Includes index.
ISBN 0-86573-755-X (softcover)
1. Landscape design. I. Creative Publishing
international.
II. Series.
SB473.D45   1999 98-49604
712' .6--dc21

Contents

DESIGNING YOUR OUTDOOR HOME

Welcome 4

Basics 6
  Rooms 8
  Front Rooms 10
  Dining Areas 12
  Spaces for Kids 14
  Passageways 16
  Sports & Fitness .18
  Hobby Spaces 20
  Recreation Areas .22
  Private Retreats 24
  Utility Spaces 26

  Elements 28
  Floors 30
  Walls 32
  Doors & Windows 34
  Ceilings 35
  Utilities & Fixtures 36
  Furnishings 38

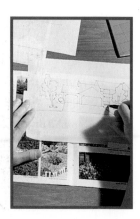

Materials 40
Wood 42
Soil & Stone 44
Manufactured Stone 46
Metals & Plastics .48

Plants 50
Annuals 52
Perennials 54
Ground Cover 56
Trees & Shrubs 57

Principles **58**
Design Concepts 60
Purpose 62
Simplicity 64
Unity 66
Balance 68
Movement 70
Interest 72
Harmony 74

Landscape Style .76
A Catalog of Traditional Styles 78

Making Plans **84**
Gathering Information 86
Brainstorming 88
Budgeting 90
Courtesies & Codes 92
The Yard Survey 96

Drawing Plans 98
Creating a Site Map 100
Sketching Bubble Plans 102
Drafting a Final Design 104
Drawing Elevations 106
Landscape Symbols 107
Creating Working Plans 108

Appendix **110**

Index **112**

Welcome

A revolution in landscape design is under way. Homeowners everywhere are beginning to discover that traditional ideas about landscaping just aren't practical anymore. Once viewed primarily as an ornamental feature, today's landscape is becoming an *outdoor home* that can include a variety of living spaces dedicated to different lifestyle activities.

The land on which your house sits contributes about 30% of the total value of your home, on average, and growing numbers of homeowners are discovering how to put this valuable space to better use. Traditional landscapes with front yards and backyards are giving way to outdoor homes that can include as many as six or seven "rooms."

If you're reading this page, it's probably because you're not satisfied with the way your yard looks or functions. Rest assured that you're not alone. Polls conducted by home improvement and landscaping magazines show that almost everyone wants to change their yard in some way. And that's no surprise, since many of our homes were landscaped by people who didn't even know us.

The best way to get the outdoor home you want is to design it yourself. And despite what you might imagine, learning to design a quality landscape is not only possible, it's also easy and fun. That's where *Designing Your Outdoor Home* comes in.

This book provides the background information and techniques you'll need to design a functional, practical, and attractive landscape. But it's not a traditional book about landscaping. It's a down-to-earth book about designing an outdoor home that serves your needs and tastes.

Designing Your Outdoor Home differs from traditional books on landscaping in three important ways.

First, we'll encourage you to design your yard so it meets your day-to-day needs rather than some set of abstract design standards. Landscapes created by professionals may be very artistic, but they aren't always practical for the people who live with them. First and foremost, a well-planned outdoor home is a landscape that satisfies your lifestyle.

Second, we'll help you learn to trust your own instincts when it comes to visual style. We'll introduce some easy, common-sense design concepts to help you understand why one landscape might appeal to you more than others, but we won't suggest that one look is necessarily better. We don't want to change your tastes; we want to help you clarify your opinions and develop your own personal style.

Third, we'll help you design and plan an outdoor home that you can build yourself, if you choose. Landscaping can be pretty expensive, and the very best way to save money is by doing the work yourself. Rather than suggesting complicated elements that only a professional could build, we'll focus on elegantly simple options suitable for any amateur landscaper.

Designing Your Outdoor Home is divided into three main sections.

Basics explains the idea behind our common-sense landscaping philosophy, and gives you important background information you'll need to move forward with your plans.

Principles presents an easy-to-understand lesson in the basic principles that good professional designers use when planning landscapes.

Making Plans leads you step-by-step through the process of creating plan drawings, from surveying and evaluating your yard, to putting the finishing touches on your final design drawing.

A word of advice before we get started: The process of planning a landscape is most rewarding if you relax and take your time. The best landscape designers advise clients to take a full year, if possible, to think about their needs and preferences before committing to a design. At the very least, allow two or three months for this important and enjoyable activity. If your region has a season in which it's too cold, rainy, or hot to work outdoors comfortably, this can be an ideal time to dream about and plan for the outdoor home in your future.

Basics

It's time to throw away your old landscape ideas and begin thinking of your yard as an *outdoor home*—an integrated living space with various "rooms" that serve different activities. If you can cultivate this outlook, planning your new landscape will be entertaining, exhilarating, and just plain fun. The planning process might be challenging at times, but neither the experience nor your landscape will be boring.

In this section, you'll find important background information that will help you plan a new landscape. You'll learn the advantages of turning a standard "front yard, backyard" landscape into a lively outdoor home with four or more distinctly different living spaces.

Then, we'll look more closely at the elements that make up the rooms of your outdoor home: the floors, walls, ceilings, utilities, furnishings, and decorations. Adopting the same language and concepts used for indoor remodeling, we'll show you how to think about landscaping in a refreshing new way.

Finally, we'll review the wide choice of materials and plants you can use to construct your outdoor home, discussing the pros and cons of each. You'll learn how to evaluate cost, durability, aesthetics, and ease of do-it-yourself installation when choosing materials for your landscape.

IN THIS SECTION

Rooms . . . . *page 8*
Elements . . . . *page 28*
Materials . . . . *page 40*
Plants . . . . *page 50*

Rooms

IN THIS CHAPTER

Front Rooms . . . . *page 10*
Dining Areas . . . . *page 12*
Spaces for Kids . . . . *page 14*
Passageways . . . . *page 16*
Sports & Fitness . . . . *page 18*
Hobby Spaces . . . . *page 20*
Recreation Areas . . . . *page 22*
Private Retreats . . . . *page 24*
Utility Spaces . . . . *page 26*

To transform an ordinary yard into an outdoor home, you'll need to begin seeing your landscape as a series of outdoor "rooms," each serving a different function for you and the members of your family. Adopting this viewpoint may stretch your imagination more than you think. For many people, a landscape is still little more than a decorative front yard with a large expanse of open grass, and a utilitarian backyard where most outdoor activities take place.

We're suggesting a much different landscape philosophy: an outdoor home based entirely on practical needs and personal tastes rather than traditional expectations. For some people, this might mean doing away with a formal front yard altogether—a concept that would have shocked suburban neighborhoods just a few years ago. Today, you might choose to use this space instead as a hobby den for pursuing favorite pastimes, a sports and exer-

cise studio, or an expansive recreation space where friends and family can socialize.

Of course, you don't have to be a complete revolutionary when designing your outdoor home. A great, innovative landscape can also retain traditional themes. If you enjoy the look of a decorative front room carpeted with grass and decorated with familiar foundation shrubs, by all means include that in your design. But plan the space in a way that is practical for you. Instead of a huge formal front yard, for example, you might think about reducing its scale to make space for other rooms as well. In today's landscape, almost anything goes, so long as the design satisfies your needs and tastes.

The design method you'll learn on the following pages is applicable to a yard of any size. If yours is a big suburban property, the landscape can include as many as eight different rooms. But even in a small urban yard, it's usually possible to include three or four distinct spaces. The smaller your yard, in fact, the more important it is to use every square foot of it wisely.

On the following pages, you'll see some examples of outdoor rooms dedicated to specific uses, and explore how the floors, walls, ceilings, and furnishings contribute to the function and ambience of the space. As you read, take mental notes about the types of outdoor rooms that appeal to you. A clear understanding of your own needs and preferences is the foundation on which you'll plan your great new outdoor home.

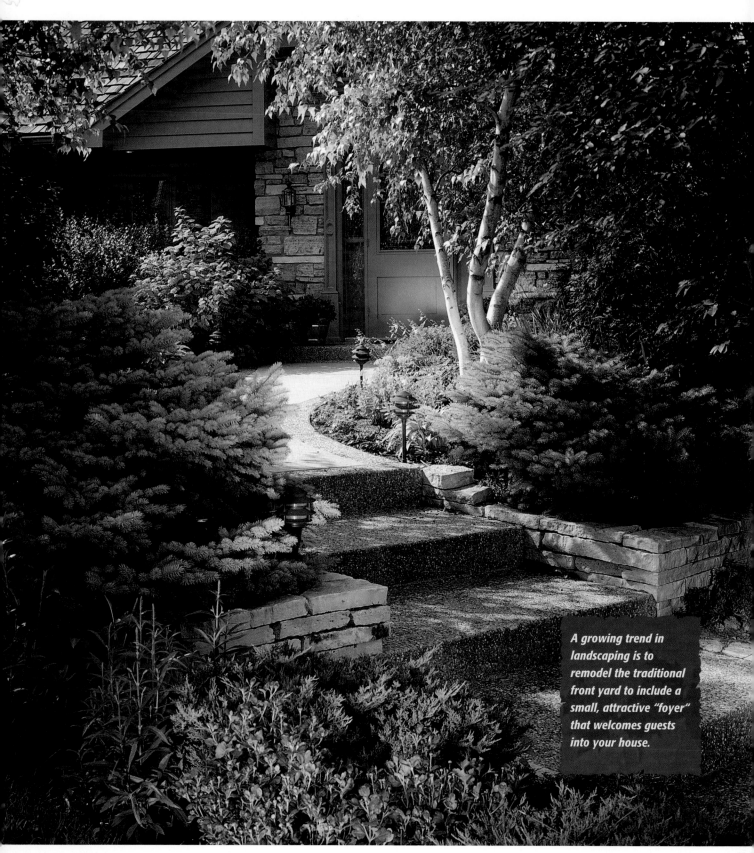

A growing trend in landscaping is to remodel the traditional front yard to include a small, attractive "foyer" that welcomes guests into your house.

Front Rooms

In many houses, the architectural design includes some type of foyer or entryway where you greet guests joined to a formal living room or parlor where you can entertain guests in style. A growing trend in landscaping is to include an outdoor front room that serves the same function: welcoming guests into your home. The front room plays a prominent role in your landscape, and it deserves careful consideration as you plan.

Floors in a large front room often consist of lawn grass or another living ground cover. Smaller front rooms are sometimes paved with durable natural stone or brick. And in some instances, the entire floor is paved to create a patio courtyard. In other landscapes, planting areas are integrated into the front room.

Walls usually enclose one or two boundaries of a front room, but the space shouldn't be completely enclosed. A front room that's completely walled off is forbidding and makes people feel claustrophobic. Walls may be solid, consisting of living hedges, garden wall, or wood screen; or they may be formed with low planting areas or beds of shrubs. The goal is to create a sense of cozy intimacy, while still providing "windows" to the surrounding landscape and neighborhood. The primary wall in a front room often includes a formal gate or archway that marks the entry to the space.

Ceilings for a front room most often consist of open sky to provide good light, but a ceiling of shade trees or wood screening can also be appropriate, especially in warm climates.

Utilities in a front room should include good lighting. Entry lighting at the door to your home can improve safety and discourage intruders. Low-voltage landscape lighting can be used to mark walkways and highlight attractive landscape features. A hose spigot or underground sprinkler system is helpful if your front room includes lawn space or planting areas that need regular watering.

Furnishings for a front room often include a simple bench or a small patio table set. A few pieces of top-quality outdoor furniture are a good investment for this room of your outdoor home.

Decorations may include ornamental shrubs and trees, and flower garden beds. One or two accent pieces, such as a fountain, statue, or birdbath, can provide focal points in a front room.

A paved courtyard is a common front room in some landscapes, such as the Mediterranean-style outdoor home.

A traditional lawn can be part of the front room in your landscape. The front lawn in today's outdoor home is often smaller than it once was, with less grass to mow and more ornamental planting areas for visual appeal.

11

A fire pit or brick barbecue provides a place to cook meals and snacks, but it can also lend a cozy atmosphere ideal for evening socializing.

Dining Areas

A welcome addition to any home is a patio or deck that extends the cooking and dining areas into the outdoors. In an outdoor dining room, even a simple meal becomes an occasion, maybe even a chance for family and friends to linger and talk.

If possible, locate the outdoor dining space adjacent to the indoor kitchen or dining room, which allows for convenient, easy movement between the spaces. If possible, link the indoor and outdoor areas with sliding patio doors or double French doors.

An outdoor cooking and dining area needs to provide about 25 square feet of area per person, and a minimum of 100 square feet. If you plan to entertain guests, plan on at least 150 square feet total. If your landscape will include a fruit or vegetable garden, you may want to position it near the outdoor kitchen.

Floors for dining areas are often carpeted with grass if informal picnicking is the norm; but wood decking, natural stone, or paver bricks are usually better choices, since these materials are durable and easy to clean. Wherever possible, choose outdoor flooring materials similar in texture or color to those used in the corresponding indoor space. Paving your patio with tiles similar to those used in the adjacent kitchen unifies the indoor and outdoor spaces, making both seem larger.

Walls should provide shelter from strong wind and direct sun, which can quickly spoil a peaceful outdoor meal. Wood screening or trellises trained with climbing plants are good choices, offering privacy, shelter, and a sound buffer.

Ceilings are common in dining areas. They can range from simple, portable umbrellas to shingled roofs. A retractable canvas awning can be a good choice, especially if you have a small yard where a permanent roof structure isn't practical.

Utilities for dining areas should include a gas or charcoal barbecue, or a brick fireplace. Include at least one electrical outlet to operate plug-in appliances. Low-voltage lighting lets you extend your dining into the evening hours. An outdoor sink makes food preparation and cleanup easier.

Furnishings should include comfortable seats and one or more dining tables. If space is limited, think about using portable fold-up furniture. A dining and food prep area also benefits from a storage space for utensils, dishes, and linens. Decorations often include planters or potted plants. Ornamental furniture made from wrought iron or teak can be used both for its function and its visual appeal.

Built-in plumbing fixtures and food preparation appliances make it more convenient to dine outdoors. Several manufacturers offer sinks, cooktops, and refrigerators designed for outdoor use.

Masonry is a classic choice for dining areas. This dining area includes a stone fireplace that is both practical and decorative.

Elaborate play houses are now available in kit form designed for do-it-yourself construction. Once the kids have outgrown this structure, it can become a storage shed, artist's studio, or private getaway for adults.

Spaces for Kids

If you have active, growing kids, devote some space to their needs and activities. Not only will the kids be happier, but you'll be more content, as well: the other rooms in your outdoor home will survive much better if one area catches the brunt of your children's exuberance. A good location for an outdoor play area is adjacent to an indoor play room. This lets kids move in and out of the house at will without disrupting the rest of the home.

Safety is an important concern, especially for small children. Try to position play areas so they are visible from the areas used by supervising adults. And keep the safety of your kids in mind when choosing construction materials and furnishings.

Kids eventually grow up, so think about how play spaces can be converted to other uses in the future. For example, a play structure can lose its kiddie swings and be used instead to hang plants and a porch swing for adults. A large sandbox used by young children can be easily converted to a fire pit when the kids reach the teenage years, then to a raised planting bed for everyone to enjoy.

Floors should be durable, but forgiving when children trip or fall. A large bed of sand or smooth pea gravel works well. Wood chips are often used, but they're not the best flooring material for these spaces, because bare feet and knees may easily pick up tiny slivers. Grass is pleasant to walk on, but it won't hold up well in areas where foot traffic is heavy.

Walls in play areas should provide security, where necessary, to keep small children in and to keep strangers and neighborhood animals out of the yard. Solid wood or chain-link fences with locking gates will make the yard secure and give you peace of mind.

Ceilings for play areas are often nothing more than a shade tree canopy that protects kids from harsh sun. Canvas awnings and wood roofs are sometimes included on timber play structures. Open sky is best for open areas where lawn games are played.

Utilities aren't essential for a play area, although lighting is a good idea if kids play outside after dark. A drinking fountain can also be a welcome addition, especially in warm, dry climates.

Furnishings often include a general-purpose play structure and storage. A chair or a bench will let you relax while supervising the kids. For older kids, you might want to include a basketball hoop, or a backstop for practicing tennis skills.

Wood timber play structures in kit form are now widely available for do-it-yourself installation. Modular styles can be upgraded with new features as your budget allows.

A sandbox is one of the least expensive play features, but it's very popular with almost all kids. A sandbox is also easy to convert to another use once children outgrow it.

Lawn grass flowing like a river through your landscape can serve as a passageway from one space to the next. It also lends unity to the landscape.

Passageways

Your outdoor rooms should have passageways connecting the various living spaces. These sidewalks, driveways, stairs, and walkways tend to receive little attention when a landscape is designed, possibly because their function doesn't seem very glamorous. In many homes, durable poured concrete is used for all passageways.

But as you design your new outdoor home, think carefully about the visual appeal of passageways and look for ways to make traditional, utilitarian sidewalks more attractive. Paver bricks or flagstones, for instance, are almost as durable as concrete, and are much nicer to look at. Ordinary concrete can be colored, and finished with a pleasing texture that resembles cobblestone.

A passageway often begins or ends with a gate, which can serve either practical and aesthetic purposes. A sturdy wood or chain-link gate provides security, while a decorative archway creates a visual invitation for visitors to explore your landscape.

Some passageways are designed primarily to serve the eye rather than the feet. The value of a stepping-stone pathway lies more in its artistic appeal than in its practical use. Passageways can also be used to create visual unity in a landscape, linking the various outdoor rooms. A river of lawn grass or a loose-fill path running in sweeping curves through your landscape serves this function.

Floors for outdoor passageways can be made of almost any building material. In a more formal landscape, poured concrete, paver bricks, or mortared natural stone is a good choice. Informal landscapes can use stepping-stones or loose-fill materials.

Walls for outdoor passageways are usually symbolic rather than structural. A basic concrete sidewalk can be edged with paver bricks or low plants, for example, to define its boundaries.

Ceilings usually aren't a big concern for outdoor passageways, though you can achieve a striking effect by enclosing a garden pathway with a tunnel-like pergola that creates both walls and a ceiling.

Utilities may include low-voltage landscape lights that improve safety and provide decoration.

Furnishings and decorations aren't essential, but a well-chosen accent—a bench or small ornamental statue, for instance—can provide an interesting focal point in a passageway.

An ideal passageway is both attractive and practical. This walkway of paver bricks arranged in a herringbone pattern is interesting to the eye, but also provides a wide, comfortable route between the garage, rear entrance, and garden.

A stepping-stone path is a good way to introduce the texture and color of natural stone into your landscape. A pathway extending out of view creates mystery and invites exploration.

A swimming pool is a great place to exercise and relax. Although a pool still represents a major investment, new materials make pools more affordable than ever. Do-it-yourself kits for in-ground swimming pools are now available for as little as $5,000.

Sports & Fitness

If physical exercise is an important part of your life, your outdoor home should be designed to serve this need. A space devoted to physical exercise can range from a patch of secluded lawn for practicing calisthenics or yoga, to an in-ground swimming pool. The types of sports you enjoy will determine the building materials and other elements you use.

Remember that many outdoor sports require a large, open space with a relatively flat ground surface. On a sloped yard, you may need to move a lot of earth to create the necessary space. The chart below gives typical space requirements for common outdoor sports.

GAME	MIN. OPEN SPACE NEEDED
• Badminton	17 ft. × 44 ft.
• Croquet	37 ft. × 85 ft.
• Tennis (singles)	50 ft. × 100 ft.
• Handball	20 ft. × 40 ft.
• Volleyball	29 ft. 6" × 59 ft.

The exact location of your exercise area will vary, depending on the activity. A swimming pool, for example, is best situated away from trees that shed leaves, in a spot where afternoon sun can warm the water. An area for croquet or badminton, on the other hand, can benefit from some afternoon shade.

Floors should be durable, especially for sports that involve lots of running, such as tennis and basketball. For sports of this type, asphalt and concrete floors are best. Lawn sports, such as boccie ball, badminton, and croquet, require a flat, well-tended lawn surface, but the spaces around a swimming pool should feature a floor of concrete, brick, or wood decking. For volleyball, a bed of sand or smooth gravel is ideal.

Walls are essential for some sports. Your local Building Code probably requires a tall protective fence if you have a swimming pool. For a tennis or basketball court, a tall chain-link fence will help keep balls in play. A wood fence can provide privacy for any sports area.

Utilities may include plumbing lines for an outdoor shower or drinking fountain, and electrical service for nighttime lighting.

Furnishings can include storage accessories, and benches or seats. Decorative accents usually aren't an important part of active sports areas.

A versatile sports court can be included if your yard has room for a large, paved area. A concrete or asphalt court can accommodate tennis, basketball, handball, shuffleboard, and other outdoor games. A variety of surface treatments are available to make a paved sports court less slippery and more durable.

A portable basketball unit can be an ideal solution where space is at a premium. These adjustable standards can be stored in the garage and rolled out onto a driveway whenever they're needed. Some models have adjustable heights.

Rooms

Butterflies and other wildlife can be drawn to your yard by the right mixture of flowers. Good plants for a butterfly garden include zinnias, asters, foxglove, marigold, lupine, butterfly weed, purple coneflower, and violets.

Hobby Spaces

If you have a favorite pastime, you probably want to dedicate a portion of the landscape to the enjoyment of that hobby. Some hobbyists—especially gardeners—devote the entire yard to their pastime. The layout of the space and your choice of features will be dictated by the nature of your hobby.

Gardening. If gardening is your hobby, you'll probably want to designate a large section of the landscape for growing plants. Areas that enjoy good soil and lots of sunlight are ideal spots. If your passion is for decorative flowers, plan your outdoor home so the ornamental garden is clearly visible from inside the house. Raised planting beds make it easier to tend plants, which is an important consideration for older gardeners or those with physical limitations. One or more storage sheds or cabinets are useful if you own many tools and supplies.

You'll almost certainly want to include water service, either in the form of an underground sprinkler system or a simple hose spigot for filling a watering can. Landscape lighting lets you enjoy the garden during the evening hours.

Wildlife study. As an animal lover, you'll want to create an outdoor home that welcomes birds, butterflies, squirrels, and other animals. Animals have much the same physical needs as humans: shelter, food, and water. Make sure to include the features that satisfy these needs—trees, shrubs, birdhouses for shelter; feeders or edible plants for food; and a pond, birdbath, or fountain for water. If possible, include seating areas where you can sit quietly and watch visiting wildlife up close.

Choose plants that appeal to your favorite animals. Butterflies and hummingbirds are drawn to bright flowers, especially red and violet annuals. Birds will be attracted by sunflowers and other flowers that produce lots of seed. Ducks and geese favor landscapes with large ponds. Squirrels and other small mammals are drawn to trees that produce nuts.

Visual arts. If you're a painter, photographer, or wood carver, your landscape should be designed with visual interest in mind. If you plan to designate yard space as a studio, make sure this outdoor room receives the soft, warm light of morning and early evening. Decorate your studio space for visual appeal, with striking plants, garden statuary, and other ornaments that can provide subject matter for your craft. If areas beyond your property are especially attractive, design your landscape so it includes "windows" that allow open views.

This outdoor passageway doubles as a showplace for a wonderfully odd and interesting assortment of collectibles.

The owners of this landscape are true animal lovers; they keep bee skeps in the garden. Bees pollinate plants and can also provide honey.

Equip your space with the furnishings and props necessary for practicing your hobby. A photographer may require electrical service to power lighting equipment, while a painter might need a classic garden bench on which models can pose. Privacy is important to many arts, which is why high garden walls or hedges are often included. You might find a small, secure shed with windows useful, both for storing equipment and materials and for providing shelter when the weather turns bad.

Recreation areas are designed with social activities in mind. Comfortable furnishings are essential to these spaces.

Recreation Areas

For many families, a recreation space devoted to social fun is the largest and most important of all the outdoor rooms. A spacious deck or patio often forms the centerpiece of this area, which may include a dining area.

Floors should be durable enough to withstand heavy foot traffic. Brick, wood, stone, and concrete are the best flooring materials. In a large outdoor recreation room, a patio or deck may open onto an expanse of open lawn where you can play croquet and other games.

Walls in recreation spaces are usually designed with privacy in mind—to preserve your own privacy as well as that of your neighbors. A living hedge or structure covered with climbing plants helps muffle noise as well as block the view. In areas where insects are a problem, a screened porch or gazebo allows you to extend your recreation time well into the night.

Ceilings for recreation areas should be chosen with your climate and lifestyle in mind.

In warm southern regions, shelter from the sun—provided either by overhead trees or artificial screens—is almost essential, while in cooler northern areas, the open sky can be a welcome ceiling year-round. In a wet climate, recreation spaces may need protective awnings or a gazebo to provide quick shelter when needed.

A large recreation space may have several different ceilings. For some activities, an open sky is the best ceiling. A poolside patio, for example, is best placed in the open rather than beneath a tree canopy. But for dining or social entertaining, a lattice screen ceiling can diffuse the sun, greatly improving your enjoyment of the space.

Utilities usually include lighting, and sometimes plumbing lines. A fire pit can be a delightful, cozy touch in climates where the evenings are cool. In a large recreation space, plumbing and electrical service may be necessary for a hot tub or swimming pool. A weatherproof sound system fed from an indoor stereo is a relatively inexpensive and easy-to-install amenity for your outdoor recreation space.

Furnishings and accents should stand up to heavy use, since recreation areas see lots of activity. Chairs, benches, and tables should be made from sturdy wood or iron. Ornamental lanterns and planters are good decorative touches for recreation areas.

A hot tub is ideal for family relaxation and small, informal social gatherings. Privacy screens can make a hot tub seem more intimate and less exposed.

A large recreation space can include unusual features, such as a putting green. Several manufacturers offer supplies and directions for installing do-it-yourself putting greens.

Rooms

Peace, quiet, and
privacy are the
hallmarks of an outdoor
room dedicated to
reflection and relaxation.
In the space shown
here, the elements are
designed to appeal to
all the senses.

Private Retreats

Socializing is a big part of our lives, and a well-planned outdoor home needs to provide space for these activities. From time to time, however, most of us need to get away from social activities and spend time alone.

If quiet relaxation and reflection appeal to you, then make sure your outdoor home includes a private retreat where you can nurture your soul. Even a small landscape can include this important space, since it's generally used by only one or two people at a time. A retreat can be as simple as a hammock strung between two trees or as elaborate as a gazebo.

Perhaps the most important feature of an outdoor retreat is privacy. In a large yard, it might be possible to literally hide your retreat from sight, but even in a smaller yard you can strive for the illusion of privacy by careful use of walls and screening plants. Privacy lends an air of mystery that encourages relaxation and meditation.

Walls for private retreats can include hedges, vine-covered trellises, wooden screens and fences, and stone garden walls. Because privacy is the goal, the walls for a private retreat are often quite tall. Softscape walls—a shrub hedge or climbing vines—are popular because they dampen sound.

Floors should be appealing, both to the eyes and to the feet. Grass or another living ground cover, natural stone, and brick are all popular choices. A decorative pathway of stone or loose-fill material can lead the way into your private retreat.

Ceilings often use a canopy of vines or trees, which provide shade and an air of mystery. Shade is an important element of most retreats, although a sun lover may opt for an open view of the sky.

Utilities may include water lines for a pond or fountain, and landscape lighting. If you prefer a more rustic atmosphere, include a fire pit in your retreat.

Furnishings should include comfortable benches or chairs, and possibly a small garden table. Also consider accessories that draw birds, butterflies, and other creatures to your landscape. Decorations should appeal to all the senses—scent and sound, as well as sight. Wind chimes, a garden statue, fragrant flowers, or a small fountain can help create a perfect personal escape. A pond with fish is particularly soothing. Oriental themes often are considered calming, which makes them a good choice for accent pieces.

A gazebo makes a good private retreat, especially on a large site where it can be truly isolated.

A unique garden bench can be the focal point for a private retreat. This custom-built bench encircles a shade tree on which flowering vines grow.

A garden shed is a practical feature, but it can also be a design element or even a symbol of romance. Husband-and-wife gardeners designed this delightful shed as a mutual anniversary gift to one another.

Utility Spaces

Most utility rooms aren't as ornamental and "romantic" as other rooms in the outdoor home, but they're just as essential to a well-balanced landscape. Just as your house has closets, a washroom, and perhaps a workshop, your landscape should have some spaces dedicated to storage and other utility functions. And with a little imagination, utility spaces can be as attractive as any other room.

By providing a space to work on essential maintenance tasks and to store tools and materials out of sight, a well-planned utility space can actually improve the look and function of your entire landscape. Some utility features, such as a garden shed or potting bench, can also serve a decorative function if they are designed to be attractive.

In many homes, a garage or basement is expected to serve all the utility needs, but it's much better if you can also designate some actual yard space to this purpose. If possible, plan outdoor utility rooms in spots that are convenient, but slightly separated from the rest of the landscape.

The space between your house and your neighbor's yard can be an ideal utility space. This area may already serve as home to a central air-conditioning unit or electrical meter and can also be used to store garbage cans, recycling containers, or a compost heap. A well-designed utility space keeps these features organized and hidden from view.

Pet spaces. Family pets—especially dogs—can have a dramatic impact on the outdoor home. Animal wastes can ruin grass and ornamental plants, and make children's play areas unhealthy and unusable. An exuberant dog can dig up expensive ornamental plants or gnaw wooden structures to pieces.

The answer to this problem is to dedicate an area of the landscape to your dog's needs. When the family is outdoors, a dog can be allowed to romp with the kids. But it's a good idea to have an area where pets can be confined and sheltered when necessary.

A standard kennel with a fence, concrete or brick floor, and a shelter is perhaps the best choice for a dog, because it is easy to clean and protects the rest of the landscape from damage. For most dogs, you can get by with an 8-ft. × 8-ft. kennel with 6-ft.-high chain-link walls, though the size of the dog obviously affects this decision.

Another alternative is to reserve a segment of your lawn for the pet. If you choose this option, it's best to fence in this area to simplify weekly cleanup chores.

This full-featured gardening center takes up little space, yet includes storage shelving, a potting bench, and compost bin. Decorative fencing hides the utility room, and gravel provides a durable, easy-to-maintain floor.

A good dog kennel has a concrete floor that's easy to clean, and chain-link walls that allow your dog an open view of the yard and provide for good air circulation.

Elements

IN THIS CHAPTER

Floors .... page 30
Walls .... page 32
Doors & Windows .... page 34
Ceilings .... page 35
Utilities & Fixtures .... page 36
Furnishings .... page 38

By now, you're beginning to think about your landscape as a connected group of outdoor rooms. Now it's time to look at the individual elements that make up those rooms.

The principles used for designing and remodeling interior rooms and outdoor living spaces are remarkably similar, even though the construction materials used can be much different. Outdoor living spaces have the same elements as indoor rooms: floors, walls, ceilings, plumbing lines, furnishings, and decorations. Anyone who has remodeled an indoor room can also successfully convert a tired landscape into a full-featured outdoor home.

In a well-planned landscape, the floors, walls, and other elements are constructed with materials that are well suited to the use of the space. One of the keys to good landscape design is choosing construction materials that are attractive as well as practical. This simple, commonsense principle is overlooked surprisingly often.

A wall of thorny shrub roses looks great—unless those walls form the boundary for a play area for small children. Here, you'd be better off with a sturdy chain-link fence planted with climbing vines—a combination that provides privacy, muffles noise, and creates a pleasant backdrop for other landscape features, such as planting beds.

A driveway made from expensive flagstone loses its appeal once heavy vehicles break the stone slabs into rubble. The more practical option might be a sturdy concrete driveway built with colored cement or finished with an attractive patterned surface.

A huge lawn punctuated with large beds of fine perennial flowers isn't very appealing if you don't have the time or interest to do yard work. In that case, a landscape with large areas carpeted with low-maintenance ground covers would suit your lifestyle better.

As you read the following pages, pay attention to how practical function and visual appeal affect your choice of elements for the outdoor home.

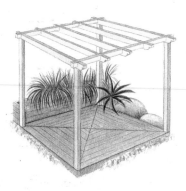

Floors

The floor of an outdoor room is one of the most prominent visual elements of a landscape, and it must also be one of the most durable. An outdoor floor is expected to tolerate heavy use—by people, pets, bicycles, or even automobiles. The choice of

A single outdoor room may use several different flooring materials to provide aesthetic variety. This setting includes stepping-stones, bark mulch, concrete, and lawn grass.

flooring is a crucial decision, so don't automatically opt for a carpet of traditional turf grass and plain concrete paving.

In reality, you have dozens of materials to choose from when planning the floors for your outdoor living spaces. Your choices will depend on many factors—cost and installation difficulty, for example. But above all else, the flooring material must be appropriate for the intended use of the space, and it should provide a neutral or complementary backdrop for the other elements of the landscape.

Lawn areas. The grass lawn has been with us for centuries, though it's now groomed by machines rather than by grazing cattle and sheep. Standard turf grass is still an excellent flooring choice for many areas of the outdoor home. It's a relatively sturdy and forgiving living ground cover that tolerates a fair amount of use from children and pets. Grass is comfortable to the feet and soothing to the eye. With its deep green color and fine texture, a healthy lawn makes a perfect backdrop for ornamental shrubs, trees, and flowers. A lawn is also relatively inexpensive, especially if you start it from seed.

But today there's no rule that your entire landscape must be covered with grass. There are good reasons to opt for other flooring surfaces.

A grass lawn requires quite a bit of regular maintenance in order to retain its healthy look; on average, about two hours per week. If lawn work isn't your idea of enjoyable exercise, consider other flooring options, or at least reduce the size of the lawn. A lawn is difficult to maintain where foot traffic is too heavy, or where it's abused by pets, children, bicycles, or other vehicles. These areas are best suited to a different flooring surface, such as stone paving or loose-fill materials. And finally, grass requires lots of sunshine and water to thrive. In shady areas of your yard, trying to grow healthy, thick turf grass is an exercise in futility. In damp climates, frequent rain can make lawn grass muddy and unusable. In areas that enjoy a good balance of sun and rain, a lawn may need to be mowed twice each week.

Ground cover. If you're set on the idea of a living floor covering, remember that you still have choices other than grass. Mosses, violets, ivies and other vines, and low-growing perennial flowers all make wonderful ground covers, especially in shady areas where grass is hard to grow. Alternative ground covers are also the best choice on irregular or sloped yards where mowing is a tricky chore.

In shady spots and other areas where grass won't thrive, don't fight the inevitable. Use an alternate ground cover, instead. In this landscape, ferns, hostas, and other shade-loving plants form the floor beneath a group of trees.

Be aware though, that some of these ground covers are a bit more tender than turf grass and will suffer if the foot traffic gets too heavy.

Loose-fill materials. Gravel, wood chips, bark, and sand are good floor coverings for many areas where grass isn't practical. Sand or smooth gravel is a durable, forgiving surface for a child's play area, and wood chips, bark, or cocoa bean mulch can be a good choice for areas that can't be mowed, such as the ground under a deck or around a group of shrubs. These materials also work well for pathways, though they should be confined by a boundary of bricks, lumber, or another edging material.

Paths & driveways. Poured concrete and asphalt are traditional flooring materials for sidewalks and driveways that receive heavy foot and vehicle traffic—and for good reason. These materials are easy to shape and can tolerate heavy use for many years without much maintenance. Paving large expanses with either concrete or asphalt is a job for professionals, however, which adds significantly to the cost. And neither asphalt nor concrete is a very attractive surface. For this reason, other materials are

growing in popularity. Manufactured paver brick, for example, provides an attractive color and texture in a landscape, and is almost as durable as concrete. Ordinary concrete can also be colored or given a decorative finish to make it more attractive. An existing concrete driveway or path can also be given a face-lift with a mortared layer of thin paver brick.

You have more options when choosing surfaces for paths. Concrete and paver brick often are used, but other possibilities include cobblestone, flagstone, gravel, sand, bark chips, or shredded wood.

In some landscapes where most of the floor surfaces are given over to other ground materials, lawn grass forms the floor for pathways running between the various living areas.

Patios. A patio or terrace paved with concrete, brick, or natural stone provides a hard, durable, easy-to-maintain floor for many outdoor rooms. It's a great choice for social spaces, in areas where basketball or tennis will be played, and as a floor surrounding a swimming pool. When built with stone or brick, a patio provides a degree of elegance that

few other flooring choices can match. But a stone or brick patio is one of the more expensive flooring choices, and building one yourself takes quite a bit of time and effort. A patio requires a perfectly flat base, so it requires extensive preparation if your yard is uneven.

A concrete patio can be attractive as well as durable. This patio includes redwood dividers and a brushed aggregate finish to create pattern and texture.

Decks. A wood deck is suitable for most of the same applications as a patio and has several advantages. A deck is generally cheaper than a stone or brick patio. It can be built on uneven or steeply sloped terrain where a patio isn't practical. A deck can also be elevated well above the ground—built adjacent to a second-story interior room, for example. A deck requires a bit more ongoing maintenance than a brick patio, but it's considerably easier to care for than a turf-grass lawn.

A deck is a perfect way to create horizontal floor space on an uneven or sloped yard. In this landscape, the natural wood finish and vertical rail pattern complement the style of the house.

Walls

Each of the rooms in your outdoor home should have boundaries that define the space. Without walls of some type, your landscape will appear random, sprawling, and impersonal. In some rooms, these walls will be literal—a fence or garden wall that creates a solid physical barrier, but in other outdoor

A low hedge makes a good transitional wall between lawn grass and planting areas. A low hedge creates boundaries without interrupting the view.

rooms the boundaries will be more symbolic. A low row of shrubs or bed of flowers can serve to separate living spaces more gently than is possible with a solid barrier.

Walls in all their various forms serve obvious practical functions, but the ornamental, aesthetic benefits are just as important. Practically speaking, a garden wall—or the modern counterpart, a fence or hedge—provides security and privacy, offers shelter from wind and sun, and muffles neighborhood noise. Retaining walls have the vital job of holding back earth on a sloped yard. Aesthetically, outdoor

---

TIP:

Many people are surprised to learn that a sturdy, solid fence doesn't do much to block strong winds. When a strong breeze hits a solid wall or fence, it surges up over the obstacle, then sharply downward, creating a swirling gust that can ruin plants. A better choice as a wind block is a hedge or staggered board fence that breaks up a strong gust into small, harmless eddies.

---

walls give you a chance to introduce new textures and patterns into your landscape. They can provide a good backdrop for decorative plants and can introduce an important vertical element into your landscape.

Traditionally, landscape walls are installed on the property lines between homes, but remember that you can also use walls to separate different living areas within your yard. A fence can screen off a utility space from the rest of the yard, for example. A trellis trained with vines can help turn a deck or patio into a quiet retreat isolated from the other sections of your yard.

It's important to remember that any solid fence or wall will block your view, as well as the views of your neighbors. When planning the walls of your outdoor home, make sure you're not sacrificing a pleasant view of the surrounding neighborhood. And it's a good idea to consult with neighbors before building a high fence or wall that will affect their view.

A brick garden wall adds a touch of elegance to any landscape. In this example, shrubs and flowers soften the transition from the wall to the lawn.

Fences. A fence is the most common wall choice for today's outdoor home, for good reason. Precut wood pieces, including pickets, rails, and even entire fence panels, are relatively cheap and easy to find at your local home center or building supply store. Metal brackets make it easy to build a basic, traditional fence, and it takes only a bit of imagination to design and build a truly unique fence.

Garden walls. A garden wall made of brick or stone is a classic landscape feature that sends a message of wealth and luxury. Properly built, a mortared stone or brick wall will last for many decades and won't require much upkeep. But a traditional 6-ft.-high garden wall built from mortared brick or stone isn't very practical for most of us. Hiring someone to build such a wall is very expensive, and doing it yourself can take literally hundreds of hours.

Roses and other flowering shrubs can create a low ornamental hedge. With its thorns, a rose hedge can also be quite effective as a security wall.

A low, curved retaining wall creates an effective border between two outdoor living spaces. A border of shrubs or flowers softens the transition.

A raised planting bed, built with retaining walls, can help define boundaries of an outdoor living space and it also introduces visual interest in a yard that is otherwise flat. This boulder retaining wall would look most natural in an informal landscape.

A healthy evergreen hedge creates privacy and serves as an elegant backdrop for decorative flower beds. However, a hedge requires regular maintenance in order to look its best.

But there are several ways to borrow some of the aesthetic appeal of a traditional mortared stone wall without the big expense. You can use natural stone to build a dry-laid wall without mortar, for example. Or, you can build a wall from decorative concrete block.

Hedges. Shrubs planted in rows can create a living wall with wonderful color and texture. Although a hedge doesn't provide the same security as a fence or garden wall, it can create a dense visual screen, and works better than a fence for diffusing wind and absorbing noise.

A hedge is more difficult to maintain than a fence, however. It needs to be watered and fertilized frequently, and must be pruned twice a year to maintain its shape. And shrubs are prone to damage from insects and diseases.

Retaining walls. A retaining wall serves several functions in a yard with a steep slope. First, it helps prevent erosion. And by turning a slope into a series of terraces, retaining walls can add usable level space to your yard. If the slope is high enough to require several narrow terraces, each of the level spaces can be planted with ornamental flowers and shrubs.

Berms. A berm is a low ridge of earth that can define the boundaries of an outdoor room. On a corner property adjacent to a busy street, for example, a berm can provide much-needed privacy and can deflect noise upward. You can plant the berm with flowers, shrubs, or trees; or top it with a fence to increase privacy.

Border gardens. A border garden is a long, decorative planting area filled with perennial and annual flowers, and sometimes ornamental shrubs. In addition to lending its beauty to your yard, a border garden creates a symbolic wall that establishes boundaries without blocking the view. In its classic sense, a border garden is positioned on the boundary between two different properties, but these days a perennial border can be used to separate spaces within the yard, as well.

A gate can serve both a practical function, as a security door, and a decorative design function.

Doors & Windows

Like the rooms inside your house, outdoor living spaces should be planned with doors, to allow people to move about, and windows that frame views to the outside world.

The form of these doors and windows depends on the nature of the walls. In a traditional fence or garden wall, the doors can be fully functional gates, and the windows can be framed openings. In a landscape where border gardens form the walls, doors can be implied by a gap between planting beds where lawn grass flows from one living space to another. Where the adjacent scenery is pleasant, you can design fully open "picture windows" that give unobstructed views of the surrounding neighborhood.

Some landscape doors are mostly decorative in function. Many archways, arbors, and pergolas are designed as doorways to greet the eye. These structures imply movement and provide a visual accent for your landscape. You can also position an archway to create a picture frame effect, outlining a decorative accent or an attractive view.

Trompe l'oeil is a classic ornamental painting technique that is enjoying renewed popularity. In modern practice, the technique usually involves painting murals of open doors or windows onto a solid fence or garden wall. Trompe l'oeil murals generally work best in small garden spaces, where they serve to make the space look larger.

Lattice screens can incorporate openings that serve as windows to the outside world. In this deck, an opening in the privacy screen draws attention to a pleasant view.

A masonry wall or fence painted with a trompe l'oeil mural can make a space seem larger. Such murals can either be quite realistic, or deliberately surreal and fantastic, like this one.

Ceilings

It's often assumed that open sky will serve as the ceiling for a landscape, but this isn't the only choice, nor is it always the best one. In a climate that is often rainy, or one that's very hot and sunny, it can be difficult to enjoy the outdoors unless there is some type of overhead shelter.

At least a portion of your outdoor home should have a ceiling that protects you from the elements. Shade trees or a vine-covered arbor can create comfortable, cooling shadows and can even absorb a light rainfall. A canvas or rigid plastic awning extending out from the house offers shade and better rain protection.

Shade trees should be selected carefully. Some trees, such as lindens and maples, will cast such dense shade that only the most shade-tolerant plants and ground covers can be grown beneath them. Other shade trees that are more airy, including locusts and ginkos, are better choices in many instances.

A screened-in porch or gazebo not only provides overhead protection, but also keeps out insects, which can be a big problem in many regions of the country. Each year, thousands of open decks are converted to screened-in porches after the homeowners grow tired of swatting mosquitoes and other pests. Such shelters can be permanent structures, or you can make use of a portable tent shelter, which can be erected whenever it's needed.

As with other landscape elements, ceilings can serve ornamental as well as practical functions. The wood framing of a pergola or arbor, for example, creates a symbolic ceiling that gives texture and pattern to the vertical dimension of a landscape.

A pergola provides a ceiling structure that gives an outdoor living space a feeling of full enclosure. The effect works well for passageways and for private retreats.

Colorful cloth strips draped across a wood frame break up direct sunlight during midday hours. When energized by a light breeze, such a ceiling adds both movement and sound to your landscape.

A gazebo provides both a ceiling and walls. In regions where mosquitoes or other flying insects are a problem, a gazebo creates a pleasant haven.

Utilities & Fixtures

You wouldn't dream of building a house without electrical service and plumbing, but you'd be surprised at how many people ignore these utilities when it comes time to design their outdoor home.

Utilities. At the very least, your landscape should include one or two hose spigots and electrical receptacles mounted on the house or garage. But better still is a landscape where most of the rooms are served with an underground sprinkler system or water spigot, and with GFCI receptacles fed by underground electrical circuits.

Without wiring and plumbing, the usefulness and convenience of your landscape is seriously limited. Including sufficient utility services in your new outdoor rooms also gives you many options for adapting the landscape as your needs change over the years.

As with most elements of the outdoor home, plumbing and wiring serve both practical and decorative functions in the landscape. Electrical service lets you power motion-sensor security lights and use electric hedge trimmers and other accessories. It can also power decorative landscape lighting and the pumps on a fountain or whirlpool tub. Underground plumbing lines let you install a drinking fountain, garden utility sink, or labor-saving sprinkler system. Plumbing can also supply water to an ornamental waterfall or pond.

Another useful utility is a natural gas line, which can fuel a cooktop, barbecue, or outdoor fireplace.

Fixtures. Many outdoor rooms serve functions that require appliances and other fixtures. Let the purpose of the room dictate your choices.

Front rooms are often served by decorative low-voltage lights. If you plan to prepare meals in your

An underground sprinkler system reduces watering chores and keeps your outdoor home green and fresh. Once found only in the yards of expensive homes, sprinkler systems now can be constructed from kits that use affordable materials and are designed for do-it-yourself installation.

Landscape lighting makes your landscape more attractive and safer at night. Installing low-voltage landscape lights is an easy and inexpensive do-it-yourself project.

Floodlights help improve security around your home and can extend the use of active spaces, such as tennis or basketball courts, into the evening hours.

outdoor home—and almost everyone does—you'll want dining areas to include the equipment that makes this possible. For occasional use, a simple portable barbecue unit may be all you need. But if outdoor dining and entertaining play a big role in your lifestyle, you'll probably need a more elaborate setup, which can include a built-in gas cooktop, refrigerator unit, a sink with running water, and storage cabinets.

Another popular fixture is a decorative brick fireplace that burns either wood or natural gas. A fireplace can be used for food preparation, of course, but it can also serve as an cozy focal point for social gatherings on cool evenings. For this reason, a recreation space often includes a fireplace or fire pit.

A whirlpool hot tub gives an added dimension to a recreation space. Other fixtures you might consider for recreation areas include ornamental light fixtures and low-voltage wiring for outdoor stereo speakers.

Ornamental light fixtures are a good choice for private retreats and hobby areas as well. These spaces are also well served by including an ornamental water feature, such as a pond or fountain.

Kids' spaces and sports areas generally don't require much in the way of appliances and fixtures, other than light fixtures to make evening use of the space practical.

A hot tub inset in a deck creates a wonderful space for relaxation or small, intimate social gatherings.

Dining areas may require electrical service, plus plumbing and gas lines. This full-featured outdoor kitchen even includes a built-in refrigerator.

Most ornamental water features require both plumbing and electrical wiring. This waterfall uses a small electric pump to recirculate the water.

Path lights can be integrated into any landscape style—formal, or rustic.

Furnishings

Once the basic elements of your outdoor living spaces are planned, it's time to turn to the furnishings and decorative accents. Furnishings play a huge role in the practical function of outdoor living spaces and, along with decorative features, they do much to influence the overall style and mood of your landscape.

Furniture. As with all the other landscape elements, the benches, chairs, tables, and other furniture in your outdoor rooms should be practical, and should help contribute to the overall style or look that you've selected.

Let common sense guide your choice of furnishings. An eating area or entertaining space almost certainly needs one or more tables and should have enough chairs or benches for family and friends. Furniture for these spaces should be durable and easy to clean. A private retreat, on the other hand, may require little more than a stylish and comfortable bench or chair. A children's play space calls for play structures and furnishings chosen for their entertainment value as well as their sturdiness and safety.

If your space and budget allow, it's best to choose durable, permanent furniture for your outdoor rooms. Stone, teak, redwood, cedar, and wrought iron are the materials of choice for permanent outdoor furnishings, because these materials are very attractive as well as durable.

But in many homes it's necessary for some outdoor rooms to serve different functions at different times of the day, which makes large, heavy pieces of furniture impractical. A wood deck might serve as a children's play space during the day, but as an adult social area at night. In these instances, portable furniture is a good option. The stereotypi-

Lounging furniture is important for recreation spaces and private retreats. A simple hammock and glider swing set the tone for this area dedicated to relaxation.

Outdoor furniture can take many forms, from a comfortable wicker rocker to a stone garden bench that lends an architectural touch to a landscape.

cal folding lawn chairs made from metal or wood are still available, of course, but new, more stylish products are quickly replacing them. New plastic-resin furniture, which is light, sturdy, inexpensive, and attractive, may be ideal for you.

Accents. If you plan well, much of the visual appeal in your landscape will come from the functional elements of your outdoor home—the wood and stone used in the walls, floors, furnishings, and so forth. But some landscape elements exist solely for their decorative appeal rather than their practical function. Your choice of accents will do much to make the landscape reflect your personality.

Flower gardens and other planting beds often serve as landscape decoration, as do potted plants, statuary pieces, wind chimes, water gardens, fountains, and other water features.

When decorating a landscape, try to appeal to all the senses—not just the visual. One of the major appeals of a water feature, in addition to the sparkling, reflected light, is the musical sound of running, splashing water. Many flowers are chosen for their scent, and wind chimes for their enchanting tones.

A large water feature, such as this pond with a fountain, makes a dramatic statement in a landscape. Such features aren't practical in every landscape. They're best suited for homes with classic styling and lots of yard space—and for homeowners with ample budgets. But there are hundreds of more modest water features that can provide the same effect when used in a small yard.

A simple birdbath can add visual appeal in many ways—as a piece of garden sculpture, as a water feature that reflects light, and as an attraction for birds. Such permanent features anchor and balance the living landscape, which changes constantly.

Baskets of flowers are a versatile way to decorate your outdoor rooms. Here, flower baskets suspended from an iron frame fill in a "wall" created by a border garden and sharpen the boundary between spaces.

Materials

IN THIS CHAPTER

Wood .... page 42
Soil & Stone .... page 44
Manufactured Stone .... page 46
Metals & Plastics .... page 48

The materials used to build the walls, ceilings, floors, and other elements of your outdoor home have far-reaching effects. These selections will influence your landscape's look and style, its durability and maintenance needs, and its overall cost.

Professional landscape designers and contractors often categorize the various materials as either "hardscape" or "softscape" materials.

Hardscape materials include those used to build the nonchanging structure of the landscape. They include natural and manufactured stone, wood, and durable plastics. Softscape materials are the living components of a landscape: the turf grass, flowers, trees, shrubs, and other plants that make up the outdoor home.

Each building material has its own qualities—both good points and drawbacks—and knowing these qualities helps you create a landscape that meets your practical needs and budget.

Keep three issues in mind when choosing the hardscape and softscape materials for your outdoor home: visual appeal, cost, and installation requirements. When planning your landscape, you'll need to constantly weigh the relative importance of these three considerations.

Although there are exceptions, it's an unfortunate truth that the most attractive building materials are usually the most expensive, as well. One way to make top-of-the-line materials more affordable is to do the installation work yourself. The cost of a cut-stone garden wall is reduced by about 40% if you build it yourself rather than have a stonemason do the work. Saving money by doing the work yourself will only be practical, however, if you feel confident of your do-it-yourself abilities.

On the following pages we'll describe the qualities of many different building materials available to you. The choices you make ultimately will be based on your personal taste, your budget, and your skills as a do-it-yourselfer.

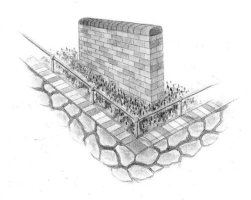

Bark mulch

Cedar bark wood chips

Teak

Cedar lattice

Redwood

Pine

Wood

Wood is perhaps the most versatile of all outdoor building materials. It can be used to form outdoor floors (decks, walkways), walls (fences, retaining walls), ceilings (pergolas and screens), outdoor furniture (benches and tables), and decorative accessories (planters and sculptures). Since it originates from living plant material, wood always looks natural in an outdoor home. It blends with almost any architectural style and looks especially good in a setting surrounded by trees. And wood is usually less expensive than stone or brick.

For do-it-yourself convenience, many precut and preassembled products are available, including posts for decks and fences; pickets, rails, and panels for fences; balusters and flooring boards for decks; and stringers and railings for stairways. You'll pay more for this convenience, but it can save you quite a bit of construction time.

Not all lumber is suitable for outdoor use. If ordinary pine framing lumber is left exposed to the elements, it will be consumed by rot and insects within a few years, in most climates. Unless you live in a very dry region, you'll need to use wood that resists these threats. Remember, though, that no wood is entirely safe from rot. Any wood left exposed to the elements requires some maintenance.

Redwood is an attractive, relatively soft wood that has natural resistance to moisture and insects. It is often used for exposed surfaces on a deck, for fences, and for outdoor furniture. Today, most redwood lumber is harvested from commercial forests rather than from old-stand forests, so you can use redwood without feeling guilty about plundering the environment. But it can be difficult to find a supplier that sells redwood at an affordable price. Few home centers carry redwood lumber, so you'll probably need to buy from a lumberyard that caters to contractors.

Cedar is another attractive soft wood that resists insects and decay. Like redwood, cedar enjoys many applications in the outdoor home, including fences, planters, decks, arbors, and screens. Cedar is also less expensive and easier to find than redwood. Most home centers carry a wide selection of cedar, both in dimensional boards and in convenient preassembled panels for fencing and screens.

When shopping for cedar or redwood, look for wood identified as "heart" or "heartwood" on the grade stamp. In both species, the heartwood, which is darker in color, has better resistance to decay than the lighter colored sapwoods.

Wood blends well with most other landscape building materials, both natural and manufactured. In this landscape, the tall privacy fence and archway successfully blend with boulder retaining walls and a decorative iron gate.

Teak and white oak are hardwoods that are sometimes used for top-of-the-line outdoor furniture. These woods, which are also used in shipbuilding, have a dense cell structure that resists water penetration. Because these woods are expensive, it isn't practical to use them for building large structures, such as a deck or fence. Instead, it's better to use these premium woods in accent pieces, such as benches or large planters.

Pressure-treated pine is the wood of choice for most outdoor construction, since it's stronger, cheaper, more durable, and more widely available than redwood and cedar. Most pressure-treated pine has a noticeable green color, but the wood can either be stained or left to weather to a pleasing gray.

Despite popular fears, the chemicals in pressure-treated pine don't easily leach into the soil, nor are they easily absorbed through the skin. But you should take some commonsense precautions when building with pressure-treated lumber: Avoid prolonged skin contact with the fresh sawdust, and avoid breathing the dust when you cut it.

Bark, wood chips, and shredded wood can be used for a loose-fill flooring surface around shrubs and in planting areas, and in pathways. In communities where a park service or urban forestry department is responsible for clearing dead trees, wood chips may be available free of charge at city collection sites.

Apply a coat of sealer-preservative or staining sealer to all sides of outdoor structures. Make sure sealer is applied to all end-grain. Even pressure-treated lumber is vulnerable to moisture and rot.

PRESERVING WOOD

Although redwood, cedar, and pressure-treated pine do resist rot, keep in mind that they won't survive indefinitely unless they are periodically treated with a good wood sealer/preservative. Choose a product from a well-known manufacturer, and apply the preservative every other year or so.

For planters, chairs, and other accessories, you can brush the sealer on. For large structures, such as a deck or arbor, it's easier to apply sealer with a pressure sprayer.

Soil & Stone

Natural stone is a classic building material for landscapes, used for everything from underground drainage systems to luxurious ornamental garden walls. Natural stone comes in a variety of forms, ranging from microscopic sands to enormous boulders weighing hundreds or thousands of pounds.

Although stone can be very important to the hardscape of your landscape, soil is even more crucial to the growth and health of grass, shrubs, trees, and other plants. The "dirt" that supports your plants is actually a complicated mixture of finely ground stone minerals, clay, silt, organic materials, and living organisms. It serves the crucial role of supplying air, water and nutrients to plant roots. Soil is also the anchor that keeps plants in place. You may be lucky enough to have plenty of good topsoil in your landscape, but it's more likely you'll need to bring in additional topsoil for various uses as you build your outdoor home.

Soil, sand, gravel, and stone are best purchased at aggregate companies and stone yards, which sell these materials in bulk at reasonable prices. Though nurseries and garden centers carry these materials, you may find the cost to be steep at these stores.

BUILDING STONE

Natural stone is one of the finest building materials you can use in your landscape. It has a beautiful natural color and texture, and a timeless elegance that no other material can match. Stone is also durable; it's not uncommon for a stone landscape wall or walkway to last longer than the home itself.

These exceptional virtues come at a price, however. Natural stone is one of the more expensive building materials you can choose. It's also very heavy, and is rather difficult to work with.

Natural stone includes a wide range of materials, ranging from rounded boulders used for building

A good stone yard is a great place to get ideas and see the types of stone that are available. This stone yard includes a display area that identifies different types of stone and suggests ways they can be used.

Dollars & Sense

TYPE	TYPICAL USE	COVERAGE	ESTIMATED COST
Limestone flagstone, 1″	Paved surfaces	150-200 sq. ft./ton	$1.50-$2.50 per sq. ft.
Granite flagstone, 2″	Paved surfaces	80-90 sq. ft./ton	$3-$4 per sq. ft.
Bluestone flagstone, 1″	Paved surfaces	140 to 160 sq. ft./ton	$2-$3 per sq. ft.
Limestone, 3″-6″ thick	Walls	20 sq. ft./ton	$7-$8 per sq. ft.
Granite , 4″ thick	Walls	20 sq. ft./ton	$12-$13 per sq. ft.
Bluestone, 2″-6″ thick	Walls	20 sq. ft./ton	$15-$16 per sq. ft.
Boulders, 6″- to 18″-dia.	Retaining walls	16 to 18 sq. ft./ton	$2.50-$3 per sq. ft.
Gravel, 4″ thick	Base for paving	50 sq. ft./ton	$15-$20 per ton
Sand, 4″ thick	Base for paving	50 sq. ft./ton	$10-$12 per ton
Black dirt, 6″ layer	Planting areas	50 sq. ft./cu. yd.	$9-$11 per cu. yd.
River rock gravel, 6″ layer	Loose fill	50 sq. ft./ton	$9-$10 per ton

retaining walls to carefully cut granite, marble, or limestone paving bricks. In its various forms, natural stone can be used in almost every element of the outdoor home, including flooring surfaces, ornamental walls, structural retaining walls, and walkways. Natural stone is also used for purely decorative features, such as rock gardens, ponds, fountains, and waterfalls.

Natural stone is sold in many different forms, so you'll need to know the following terms when you visit your local stone dealer.

Fieldstone, sometimes called *rubblestone*, is any loose stone collected from the earth's surface, rather than extracted from a quarry. Fieldstones can range in size from massive boulders to relatively small stones picked up from a river bed or field (only with permission, of course). Small, round fieldstones used for paving floor surfaces are known as *cobblestones*.

When purchased from a stone yard, fieldstone is usually sorted according to size, shape, and color. Fieldstone can be used to build retaining walls, ornamental garden walls, and rock gardens, where it creates an informal, natural look.

Cut stone refers to pieces of granite, marble, or limestone that have been cut to roughly square surfaces and edges. At some stone yards, these rocks will be known as *ashlars* or *wall stones*. Cut stone works well for stone garden walls, either mortared or dry-laid. It is quite expensive, however, so the use of cut stone is sometimes limited to a decorative cap placed atop a brick or concrete block wall.

Flagstone is uncut sedimentary rock with naturally flat surfaces. Some stone yards refer to these stones as *steppers*. Flagstone is used mostly for patios and walkways, and for stepping-stones. It can be dry-set, or installed with mortar. Limestone, sandstone, slate, and shale are the most common types of flagstone.

GRAVELS & SANDS

Gravel consists of small aggregate stone sold in bulk. It is sorted according to color, size, and stone type for a variety of different landscape purposes, both structural and decorative. Limestone- or sandstone-based gravel is used to form a base layer under concrete, asphalt, or brick paving. It's also used as an informal driveway or pathway surface.

Quartz- or granite-based gravels can be used as a loose-fill surface for informal pathways, where it lends a pleasing color and texture to the landscape.

River rock is quartz or granite gravel that has been smoothed by running water. It's generally used for decorative purposes, often as a flooring surface under a deck or bed of shrubs. It also makes a good surface for pathways. River rock that's been screened to include very small pieces of aggregate is called *pea gravel*, an ideal flooring surface for children's play areas.

Sand is actually nothing more than natural stone reduced to very small crystals through millions of years of weathering. If you examine a handful of sand under a microscope, you'll see that it consists of fine particles of granite, quartz, limestone, and other minerals. Sand is used to form a base drainage layer under patios, walkways, and driveways, and as a loose-fill flooring material for children's play areas. Like gravel, sand is available in different forms for different uses. Fine silica sand is preferred for children's sandboxes, while coarser sand provides one of the ingredients in poured concrete.

Interlocking
retaining wall
blocks

Molded
paver slabs

Exposed aggregate
paver slabs

Paver
bricks

Concrete
paver slabs

Manufactured Stone

Manufactured stone offers certain advantages over natural stone that make it a better choice for many applications. Concrete and brick are almost always cheaper than natural stone, and they are more uniform and easier to work with. Although traditional poured concrete isn't as attractive as natural stone, there are new masonry materials that can rival natural stone for elegant visual appeal.

CONCRETE BLOCKS & BRICKS

Concrete blocks and bricks are available in a growing selection of sizes and styles for use in your outdoor home. Many of these products are well suited for do-it-yourselfers, because their weights are manageable and installation is easy, though time-consuming.

Decorative block is used to make screen walls and is available in several colors. A decorative block wall is one of the most economical choices for a stone landscape wall.

Concrete paver slabs, available in several shapes and sizes, can be used for laying simple walkways and patios. They're available with a standard finish, with a smooth aggregate finish, or colored and molded to resemble brick. Concrete paver slabs are relatively inexpensive and quite easy to work with. They're usually laid in a bed of sand and require no mortar. The surface is generally finished so the smooth gravel aggregate is exposed.

Paver bricks resemble traditional kiln-dried clay bricks, but are more durable and easier to install. Paver bricks are available in a variety of colors and geometric shapes for paving patios, walkways, and driveways. They have largely replaced clay bricks for landscape use, and can be set into a bed of sand with no mortar required.

Edging blocks are precast in different sizes for creating boundaries to planting areas, lawns, and loose-fill paths.

POURED CONCRETE

A long-standing favorite for driveways, walkways, and patios, poured concrete has obvious landscape applications. It's much less expensive than natural stone, and because it's poured while in a semi-liquid state, concrete can be formed to fit curves and other shapes, such as a large landscape pond or fountain. Concrete is also exceptionally strong.

Dollars & Sense

Use the following chart as a guideline for estimating the cost of various paving materials. These costs are for materials only and assume you're doing the installation yourself. Having a professional install the materials will add to the cost.

MATERIAL	COST	DIY LEVEL
Poured concrete path or patio, 3″ thick	$.75 to $1 per sq. ft.	Moderate
Poured concrete driveway, 6″ thick	$1.50 to $2 per sq. ft.	Difficult
Concrete paver slabs, sand-set	$2 to $3 per sq. ft.	Easy
Concrete paver brick, sand-set	$2.50 to $3.50 per sq. ft.	Easy to moderate
Decorative block garden wall	$6 to $10 per sq. ft.	Moderate to difficult
Concrete edging brick	$.80 to $1.20 per linear ft.	Easy

Concrete is often criticized for its harsh, industrial look. But these days it's possible to tint concrete or give it a decorative surface finish that makes it quite attractive in a landscape.

For walkways and small paving projects, you'll probably find it easy enough to pour and finish concrete yourself. Large surfaces are more challenging, however. For a large driveway, for example, you may want to hire professionals to do the work.

When building with concrete, you have several choices. For small jobs, it's easiest to buy premixed bags of concrete, which you simply mix with water. For larger jobs, you may want to rent a power mixer and blend your own concrete using gravel and sand, bags of Portland cement, and water. For very large jobs, it's best to order premixed concrete from a local dealer. Concrete is priced and delivered by the cubic yard. The cost for premixed concrete ranges from $80 to $100 in most regions. Use this chart to estimate how many cubic yards of concrete you'll need:

Poured concrete can be colored and molded to resemble paver brick or natural stone. Many concrete contractors offer this service, but there are also kits that let you do it yourself.

SLAB THICKNESS	COVERAGE/CUBIC YARD
3″	110 sq. ft.
4″	80 sq. ft.
6″	55 sq. ft.

A sand-set brick paver patio is a project most patient do-it-yourselfers can tackle successfully. It's a time-consuming project, but not difficult.

Annuals

Annuals are plants that complete their life cycle in a single year. Growing annuals is a little more time-consuming than growing perennials, because they must be replanted every year. But annuals offer one major advantage: they provide spectacular, long-lasting color in the landscape. Unlike most perennial species, which have a peak bloom season lasting just a few weeks, many annuals bloom for virtually the entire growing season.

In addition, most annuals are rather easy to grow from seed. Not only is this an inexpensive way to grow plants, but it makes it possible to experiment with plant varieties available only through mail-order seed distributers. Most local nurseries carry a limited number of best-selling varieties, but there are hundreds or even thousands of options when you purchase seeds by mail.

Because they're not expected to live through winters, annuals usually don't carry a zone rating. Some flowers grown as annuals in northern climates are actually perennials in other regions, where the climate allows them to live through the winter. Geraniums, for example, are normally grown as annuals in cold climates, but are grown as perennials in climates where there is no killing frost. Some annuals, on the other hand, self-seed very easily where soil conditions are right. Since these annuals never need to be replanted, they are sometimes treated as perennials.

ANNUALS THAT SELF-SEED EASILY

Bachelor's button (*Centaurea*)

Cosmos

Flowering tobacco (*Nicotiana*)

Hollyhock (*Alcea*)

Larkspur (*Consolida*)

Love-in-a-mist (*Nigella*)

Marigold (*Tagetes*)

Poppy (*Papaver*)

Salvia

Snapdragon (*Antirrhinum*)

Sunflower (*Helianthus*)

Sweet alyssum (*Lobularia*)

Recommended Annuals

TEN GOOD ANNUALS FOR SUNNY AREAS WITH MOIST SOIL

Plant	Height	Color	Comments
Marigold (*Tagetes*)	1 to 4 ft.	Yellow, orange, red	Easy to grow from seeds
Petunia	1 to 2 ft.	Many colors	Thrives in almost any soil
Snapdragon (*Antirrhinum*)	1 to 2 ft.	Many colors	Also tolerates partial shade
Love-in-a-mist (*Nigella*)	12 to 18"	Blue-purple	Blooms late into autumn
Cupflower (*Nierembergia*)	6 to 15"	Purple	Perennial in the South
Hollyhock (*Alcea*)	5 to 9 ft.	Pastel flowers	Easy to grow from seed
Larkspur (*Consolida*)	1 to 4 ft.	Mauve, blue, white	Excellent for cut flowers
Geranium (*Pelargonium*)	9" to 3 ft.	Red, white, purple	Perennial in zone 10
Canterbury bells (*Campanula*)	2 to 4 ft.	Pink, blue, purple	Long-lasting blooms
Dahlia	1 to 6 ft.	Many colors	Perennial in zone 10

TEN GOOD ANNUALS FOR SUNNY AREAS WITH DRY SOIL

Plant	Height	Color	Comments
Nasturtium (*Tropaeolum*)	1 to 8 ft.	Bright yellow or orange	Good climber on trellises
Cosmos	2 to 7 ft.	Pink, yellow, orange, or white	Fernlike foliage
Moss rose (*Portulaca*)	2 to 6"	Many colors	Good in rock gardens
Alyssum (*Lobularia*)	4 to 8"	White, pink, or lavender	Fragrant blossoms
Cleome	3 to 5 ft.	Pink	Good background plant
Flowering tobacco (*Nicotiana*)	1 to 3 ft.	Pink, white	Fragrant; tolerates moist soil
Bachelor's button (*Centaurea*)	1 to 2 ft.	Purple, white, or pink	Good for cut flowers
Oriental poppy (*Papaver*)	1 to 4 ft.	Orange-red, white, red, or pink	Good in mixed borders
Scarlet salvia	1 to 3 ft.	Lavender or red	Tolerates alkaline soil
Larkspur (*Consolida*)	2 to 4 ft.	Blue, rose, or white	Good for cut flowers

FIVE GOOD ANNUALS FOR SHADY AREAS WITH DRY SOIL

Plant	Height	Color	Comments
Forget-me-not (*Myosotis*)	5 to 8"	Blue, pink, or white	Good for rock gardens
Larkspur (*Consolida*)	2 to 4 ft.	Blue, rose, or white	Won't tolerate deep shade
Honesty (*Lunaria*)	2 to 3 ft.	Purple	Tolerates alkaline soil
Browallia	1 to 2 ft.	Purple or white	Also tolerates moist soil
Bachelor's button (*Centaurea*)	1 to 2 ft.	Pink, blue, purple, or white	Won't tolerate deep shade

FIVE GOOD ANNUALS FOR SHADY AREAS WITH MOIST SOIL

Plant	Height	Color	Comments
Impatiens	6" to 2 ft.	All colors except green, blue	Prolific bloomer
New Guinea impatiens	1 to 2½ ft.	Many colors	Tolerates partial sun
Browallia	1 to 2 ft.	Purple or white	Good in container gardens
Wax begonia	6" to 1 ft.	Red, pink, or white	Tolerates acidic soil
Pansy (*Viola*)	6" to 1 ft.	Many colors	Won't tolerate deep shade

Plants

Perennials

Perennials are plants that live more than one year. Turf grasses, trees, and shrubs are all perennials, but the term usually refers to a large group of ornamental flower species. When choosing perennials for your landscape, it's important to pick plants that are "hardy" for your region and can survive the winter. For convenience, perennials are categorized according to the USDA climate zone map. Make sure you choose plants with a hardiness rating that is no lower than your temperature zone. If you live in zone 5, for example, you can grow plants rated for zones 2 through 5, but plants rated for zones 6 through 10 may not survive your winters.

The best source for perennials is a good local nursery, which will be certain to carry only those plants that are hardy in your region. Perennials can also be purchased from mail-order suppliers, but mail-order catalogs sometimes exaggerate the zone hardiness ratings to increase sales. If you purchase by mail order, first check with local nurseries or a university arboretum to make sure the plants are truly hardy in your climate.

In general, perennial flowers require less work than annuals, since they return each spring and don't need to be replanted. But it's important to remember that perennials, too, have an average life expectancy. Some (known as biennials) rarely last more than two years, while other perennials can last for many decades. If you seek a low-maintenance landscape, pick perennials known for their long lives.

In general, perennials aren't as showy and colorful as annuals, and have a shorter bloom period. A perennial border offers subtle, elegant beauty that is quite different from the dramatic display of a bed of annual flowers. Serious gardeners generally prefer perennials over annuals.

BULBS

Bulbs are a class of spectacularly colorful perennial flowers that are planted from a thickened root structure rather than from seed. The term "bulb" is used to describe a variety of root structures, including true bulbs (tulips, daffodils), tubers (begonia), corms (gladiolus), and rhizomes (iris). Many of these plants are available in potted form, but it's cheaper to buy bulbs in bulk and plant them yourself. Reputable mail-order suppliers are good sources for quality bulbs.

Like other perennial plants, bulbs are rated for hardiness according to temperature zone. If you plant bulbs that are not hardy in your zone, you'll need to either dig them up and store them each fall, or resign yourself to planting new bulbs each year.

Recommended Perennials

FIVE GOOD PERENNIALS FOR SUNNY AREAS WITH MOIST SOIL

Plant	Zone	Height	Comments
Monkshood (*Aconimum*)	2	3 to 5 ft.	Blooms late summer, fall; tolerates shade
Daylily (*Hemerocallis*)	3	1 to 4 ft.	Blooms early to late summer; tolerates partial shade
Siberian iris (*Iris siberica*)	3	2 to 4 ft.	Blooms early summer; attractive grasslike foliage
Bellflower (*Campanula*)	3	6" to 3 ft.	Long bloom season; many species available
Garden phlox	4	3 to 4 ft.	Blooms summer, early fall; easy to grow; long-lived

FIVE GOOD PERENNIALS FOR DRY, SUNNY AREAS

Plant	Zone	Height	Comments
Dianthus (pinks, carnations)	2	6" to 2 ft.	White, pink, or red blooms, early summer to fall
Black-eyed susan (*Rudbeckia*)	3	2 to 4 ft.	Gold blooms in summer; good cutting flowers
Purple coneflower (*Echinacea*)	3	1 to 3 ft.	Purple blooms in summer; good cutting flowers
Stonecrop (*Sedum*)	3	6" to 3 ft.	Blooms spring or fall; attractive foliage; long-lived
Coreopsis	4	1 to 3 ft.	Blooms spring to late summer; tolerates heat

FIVE GOOD PERENNIALS FOR SHADY AREAS WITH DRY SOIL

Plant	Zone	Height	Comments
Periwinkle (*Vinca*)	2	6 to 12"	Blooms spring to early summer; good ground cover
Foxglove (*Digitalis*)	4	2 to 4 ft.	Blooms in midsummer; tolerates clay soil
Fern (various species)	3	2 to 5 ft.	Tolerates deep shade; spreads quickly
Cranesbill (*Geranium*)	2	6 to 18"	Blooms late spring, summer; good for woodland gardens
Spotted nettle (*Lamium*)	3	6" to 1 ft.	Blooms late spring to summer; good ground cover

FIVE GOOD PERENNIALS FOR SHADY AREAS WITH MOIST SOIL

Plant	Zone	Height	Comments
Astilbe	4	2 to 4 ft.	Blooms early to midsummer; good near water gardens
Bleeding Heart (*Dicentra*)	3	2 to 3 ft.	Blooms late spring to early summer; good cut flower
Hosta	3	6" to 3 ft.	Grown for foliage rather than flowers; very long-lived
Cardinal flower (*Lobelia*)	2	3 to 4 ft.	Blooms early to late summer; good in marshy areas
Cranesbill (*Geranium*)	2	6 to 18"	Blooms late spring, early summer; good in woodlands

FIVE GOOD BULBS FOR SPRING BLOOMS

Plant	Zone	Height	Comments
Tulip (*Tulipa*)	3-8	8 to 24"	Many varieties available; good planted in masses
Daffodil (*Narcissus*)	4	up to 18"	Many varieties available; naturalizes in lawns
Hyacinth (*Hyacinthus*)	5	10"	Very fragrant; bright, unusual flowers
Crocus	3	2 to 8"	Earliest of all bulbs; can be naturalized in lawns
Bulb iris (*Iris reticulata*)	5	4 to 20"	Delicate, colorful blooms; attractive, grasslike foliage

FIVE GOOD BULBS FOR EARLY- TO MIDSUMMER BLOOMS

Plant	Zone	Height	Comments
Asiatic lily (*Lilium x*)	3	2 to 5 ft.	Long bloom period; long-lasting bulbs
Giant allium	4	3 to 5 ft.	Huge lavender flower balls; good filler for background
Tuberous begonia	10	9 to 8"	Spectacular blooms, many colors; does well in shade
American lily (*Lilium x*)	4-8	4 to 8 ft.	Red, pink, orange, and yellow blooms
Gladiolus	9	2 to 4 ft.	Blooms 8 to 10 weeks after planting

FIVE GOOD BULBS FOR LATE SUMMER AND FALL BLOOMS

Plant	Zone	Height	Comments
Oriental lily (*Lilium x*)	3	3 to 7 ft.	Spectacular blooms; very fragrant
Gladiolus	9	2 to 4 ft.	Must be dug and stored for winter in cooler climates
Caladium	10	8" to 2 ft.	Tolerates shade; dig and store for winter in cool climates
Tiger lily (*Lilium lancifolium*)	3	4 to 6 ft.	Orange flowers spotted with purple; very easy to grow
Freesia	9	1½ to 2 ft.	Many colors; blooms 10 weeks after planting

Ground Cover

In most outdoor homes, large portions of the floor areas are carpeted with turf grass or another living ground cover. These low-growing perennial plants tolerate a certain amount of foot traffic, though some species are more durable than others in this regard. On steep slopes and in other problem areas that receive little foot traffic, low-growing shrubs or larger perennials plants, such as daylilies, can be used as a ground cover.

TURF GRASS

Turf grass is the most popular living ground cover, but it has very specific cultural needs that must be met in order for the lawn to thrive:

• A grass lawn generally needs at least four hours of direct sun each day. Areas that receive less direct sunlight than this should be planted with another ground cover. In cooler, wetter climates, grass does very well with day-long sun exposure, while in hotter, dryer climates, a grass lawn may be baked unless it gets a few hours of shade each day.

• A grass lawn doesn't do well where foot traffic is very heavy, such as

Any plant with a low, mat-forming growth habit can serve as a living ground cover. In this landscape, fragrant thyme adds pleasing color and texture to an outdoor floor.

GROUND COVERS FOR SHADY AREAS

• Pachysandra
• Ajuga (bugleweed)
• Hosta
• Lamium
• Periwinkle (*Vinca*)
• Wintercreeper (*Euonymus*)
• Lilyturf (*Liriope*)

GROUND COVERS FOR SLOPES

• Daylily
• Crown vetch (*Coronilla*)
• Rugosa rose (*Rosa*)
• Creeping juniper (*Juniperis*)
• English ivy (*Hedera*)
• Virginia creeper (*Parthenocissus*)

children's play spaces or natural pathways across the yard.

• A grass lawn needs a fair amount of water. If you want to grow a lawn in a dry climate, you must be prepared to irrigate frequently or install a sprinker system.

If your conditions are suitable for grass, you have two options for creating a lawn. Laying rolls of commercially grown sod gives you faster results, but planting grass seed is much cheaper. In arid climates where sod must be grown in a controlled environment, a sod lawn can be prohibitively expensive. Creating a lawn by seed also allows you to pick grass species that will do well in special conditions, such as in deep shade or in play areas that are used heavily.

OTHER GROUND COVERS

Alternative ground covers are the best choice where heavy shade or other conditions make it hard to grow grass. There are several good ground covers that thrive in shade and never require mowing.

Increasingly, homeowners are opting for ground covers other than grass, even where there is plenty of sun to support a lawn. If you have a steep slope that's difficult to mow, or if you simply dislike lawn work, consider covering the floor areas of your outdoor home with a different ground cover. Remember, though, that few ground covers tolerate foot traffic as well as turf grass.

Trees & Shrubs

Shrubs and trees are a class of perennial plants that have woody stems. They serve obvious practical functions in the outdoor home—trees provide a ceiling of shade; shrubs create privacy walls. But trees and shrubs also serve important decorative functions. Flowering shrubs and trees add bright color, while evergreens contribute mass and shape to the overall composition of your outdoor home.

Shrubs and trees are categorized as either *deciduous* or *evergreen*. Deciduous trees and shrubs lose their leaves each fall and grow new leaves in the spring. Many deciduous trees and shrubs provide vibrant fall color just before shedding their leaves. Evergreens keep their leaves year-round, and help provide color and mass to the winter landscape.

It's crucial that you think about the mature size of the trees and shrubs you're considering. One of the most common landscaping mistakes is to plant trees and shrubs too close together, or too close to buildings and other structures. Ornamental trees planted next to your home's foundation may look fine for a few years, but eventually they'll outgrow the site, blocking light to your windows and possibly damaging your foundation. When planning the location of trees and shrubs, make sure to position them as though they're already full grown.

The distinction between trees and shrubs is not always clear. Some plants sold as shrubs require regular pruning to keep them from becoming small trees. Before you purchase trees and shrubs, make sure you understand the care and maintenance needs of the varieties you are considering.

You'll have several options for purchasing trees and shrubs for your landscape.

Bare-root plants have had the soil removed from their roots after being dug from the ground. They're generally purchased and planted in the spring before the leaves appear and are less expensive than plants sold in containers. Mail-order sources usually sell only bare-root plants, since they can be shipped at reasonable expense. Bare-root plants require careful planting, however.

Container plants are sold in the pots in which they have been grown. Available throughout the growing season, container specimens can be planted any time the soil can be worked. Container-grown trees are relatively inexpensive, but it takes quite a while for them to achieve good size.

Many ornamental trees and shrubs create beautiful spring color. Shrubs and trees also add shape and definition to a landscape.

Balled-and-burlapped plants, also called B & B, have had their roots pruned to form a compact fibrous root ball that is wrapped in burlap. B & B plants are sold throughout the growing season and can be planted any time the soil can be worked. B & B trees and shrubs are generally larger (and more expensive) than container-grown plants and will reach adult size relatively soon.

Spade-planted trees are mature plants that are dug and planted with a large tree-spade machine. Spade-planted trees are a good option if you want a mature-looking landscape immediately. Spade-planted trees cost hundreds or even thousands of dollars, however. For this reason, most people find it practical to invest in just one or two spade-planted trees for important locations in the landscape, then use B & B or container-grown plants for other areas.

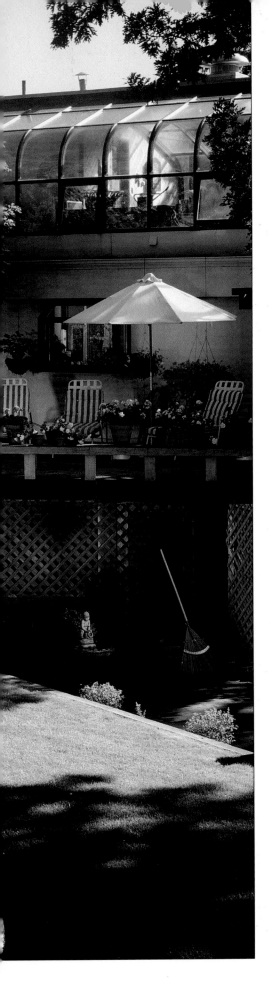

Principles

This section of *Designing Your Outdoor Home* will give you a quick but comprehensive introduction to the artistic, or aesthetic, principles that professional artchitects and designers use when planning residential landscapes. With these insights, you'll be ready to begin the rewarding and fun process of creating plan drawings for your new outdoor home.

Don't be intimidated by the idea that you'll be serving as your own landscape designer. Although landscape professionals are highly trained specialists in their fields, much of their knowledge is based on principles and concepts that almost anyone can understand and apply. You'll be surprised at just how many design principles are based on good old-fashioned common sense.

In the first chapter, "Design Concepts," you'll learn seven simple concepts that will help guide your landscape planning decisions. Applying these principles makes it quite easy to design a successful landscape.

In "Landscape Styles," you'll see how a landscape can be designed around certain popular themes that create a unified look. Choosing a thematic style makes it easier to choose the best materials, plants, landscape structures, and layout for your outdoor home. The chapter includes a short catalog of popular landscape styles that you can use as a guide for designing your own landscape.

IN THIS SECTION

Design Concepts . . . . *page 60*
Landscape Styles . . . . *page 76*

Design Concepts

IN THIS CHAPTER

Purpose . . . . page 62
Simplicity . . . . page 64
Unity . . . . page 66
Balance . . . . page 68
Movement . . . . page 70
Interest . . . . page 72
Harmony . . . . page 74

Over the years, architects and designers have learned that people are more likely to enjoy landscapes that are composed and decorated using certain familiar patterns and themes. You probably already understand many of these design concepts, even if you've never heard labels attached to them.

Whenever you spot a landscape that you instantly enjoy, take a minute to identify the elements that please you. Maybe it's the complementary blues and yellows in a perennial flower bed, or the texture and sweeping lines of brick walkways and edgings. Perhaps it's the creative use of space, or the consistent use of stone throughout the landscape. Once you understand why certain yards appeal to you—and why others don't—you'll be in a good position to plan your own outdoor home.

Don't be intimidated by complicated terms such as "axis," "rhythm," "line," and "nucleus" that you might hear from landscape experts. In reality, all those lofty terms can be summarized by a handful of simple, commonsense ideas we'll talk about on the following pages: *purpose, simplicity, unity, balance, movement, interest,* and *harmony.* If you keep these seven ideas in mind while designing and planning your outdoor home, success is almost guaranteed.

Initially, you may find that two or three of these design principles ring especially true, while others aren't quite as clear. If this is the case, then just focus on the concepts that are most meaningful to you, and don't worry about the rest. As you work on your design ideas, these other principles will gradually become more understandable.

And don't worry if some of the principles in this chapter seem to contradict one another at first. At one point, for example, we'll say that a landscape should be simple, restrained, and unified, while on another page we tell you that variety makes a landscape more interesting. Be patient. Later, as you work toward a final design for your landscape, you'll begin to see that these principles don't disagree at all, but serve to complement one another. In a very simple landscape design, for instance, you might choose to build all the features with natural stone, but you can still include variety by using a strikingly different type of stone in one or two places.

A final word: Don't feel obliged to follow any set of design "rules" when planning your outdoor home. The only goal is to create an outdoor home that expresses your personality and suits your lifestyle.

Purpose

The single most important design principle is that of function, or *purpose*. It's also the principle most often neglected. A professionally designed landscape can be visually stunning, but fail nonetheless because it doesn't serve the owner's needs.

Each separate space or "room" in your outdoor home should be designed to fulfill one or more definable purposes or goals. For an entry space leading to the front door of your home, the purpose might be simple visual appeal. For a secluded backyard patio, the primary goal might be privacy.

Knowing the intended purpose of a space is crucial to the planning process. A deck used primarily for subathing, for example, should be

Well-chosen furnishings can help define the purpose of an outdoor living space.

placed where it will receive afternoon sunlight, while a deck used for family meals and entertaining is enhanced by positioning it to enjoy the shade of an overhanging tree.

As you design the various rooms of your outdoor home, consider the purpose of each space and make a list of the elements that will help fulfill that function. A play area for young children, for example, might require a location that is visible to supervising adults; a forgiving flooring surface, such as smooth gravel; a secure fence or wall that prevents youngsters from wandering off; trees or an awning that provides sheltering

Shelter, security, and proximity to adult supervision are important for children's play areas.

shade; and play equipment and furnishings that appeal to kids.

Remember, too, that some outdoor living spaces have more than one purpose. An expansive front yard area may serve as decoration much of the time, but may occasionally be the site for yard games or social gatherings. And the purpose of an outdoor room may change over time—from season to season, or over several years. A summer patio can become a winter room for bird-watchers. Or a children's play area can be turned into a gardener's hobby area after the kids are grown. Recognizing that the purpose of an outdoor room may change over time helps you plan your landscape effectively.

Space. Make sure the physical size of the space is suitable for the purpose. Except for utility spaces, any outdoor room that receives regular use should provide a minimum of 100 square feet of space. Even a space used by only one or two people won't be comfortable unless it is roughly 10 ft. × 10 ft. or larger in size. But it's also a mistake for an outdoor room to be too large. A very large deck or patio, for example, can make people feel lost unless it is subdivided to provide smaller, more intimate areas.

Boundaries. In a well-planned landscape, clearly defined boundaries separate the living areas. Sometimes these boundaries are formed by physical barriers, such as fences or walls. But boundaries can also be implied by a curving row of low shrubs, or a bed of flowers. Yards without boundaries between areas seem aimless and lacking in purpose.

Transitions. Give special attention to the transitions between outdoor rooms. Smooth, gradual bound-

Brick edging creates an effective transition between a lawn and perennial flower garden, and also simplifies maintenance by making the lawn easier to mow.

aries are more pleasing than abrupt transitions. For example, the transition between a concrete slab and a grass lawn can be much improved with a narrow bed of perennial flowers or shrubs, or with an edging of paver bricks. Good designers understand that abrupt transitions between materials are moderated by the addition of a third material.

Shelter. Depending on the climate in your region, an outdoor room may require shelter from sun, wind, rain, or insects in order to fulfill its purpose. In some regions, a simple canopy of trees or an awning extending from the house may provide all the shelter you need, while in other areas, a gazebo with a shingled roof and insect screens may be necessary.

Utilities. Some spaces in your outdoor home may require electrical and plumbing lines. A deck or patio without lighting won't function very well for

nighttime social gatherings. And a flower garden without a plumbing line for watering the plants isn't very practical. You may also want to consider telephone, television, and sound system wiring for some of your outdoor rooms.

Utilities, such as a sprinkler system, plumbing line, or electrical circuit can be crucial to the function and purpose of an outdoor room.

With its simple elegance, this front room perfectly serves its purpose: to greet and welcome guests into the home.

Unity

As a design principle, the term *unity* refers to the art of making a landscape fit in visually with its surroundings. A good landscape complements not only your home, but the surrounding neighborhood and the larger community as well. Unity makes a landscape seem natural and creates a more comfortable, reassuring environment. In addition to being unified with its surroundings, your outdoor home should have internal unity—the individual rooms of your landscape should complement one another.

SOME GUIDELINES FOR ACHIEVING UNITY:

• Build your landscape using building materials also used in your home. If your house is made of brick, for example, use brick for paved surfaces and garden walls. If it's not practical to use exactly the same materials, try to select materials with colors that match those found in the house. On a house with brown roof shingles, for example, you might build a retaining wall with sandstone or interlocking block in a matching shade of brown. If your house has Victorian detailing, you might copy some of these ornamental touches in the design of a wood fence and gate.

• Use repetition to unify the rooms of your outdoor home. Making sure that adjacent outdoor spaces share colors or patterns will help to visually unify your landscape. An informal hallway of stepping-stones running between adjacent rooms is another way to create unity. Or, you can repeat key shrubs or flowering plants from room to room. A classic way to create this unity is by using a continuous carpet of lawn grass flowing from one outdoor living space to the next.

• Use rock and wood products that are indigenous to your region. These materials will be familiar and easy to obtain in your area, and using them will

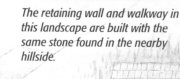

The retaining wall and walkway in this landscape are built with the same stone found in the nearby hillside.

This landscape features steps and retaining walls built from brick that matches the materials used in the house. This is an excellent way to create unity.

make your landscape seem natural. If you live in a mountainous region, for example, a retaining wall built from granite boulders will seem more natural than one built from sedimentary sandstone. In addition, indigenous materials are likely to be cheaper than those imported from far away.

• Pay attention to transitions between the house and yard, between the different rooms of the landscape, and between your landscape and adjacent properties. If you can make these transitions gradual rather than abrupt, you'll have done much to im-

Good designers understand that abrupt transitions between materials are moderated by the addition of a third material. In this yard, a low hedge improves the transition between lawn grass and concrete paving.

prove the sense of unity. A well-planned foundation planting of shrubs and flowers, for instance, is essential for unifying the house with the rest of the landscape.

• Repeat the decorating scheme of your indoor home. If the interior of your home is decorated in a Colonial style, for instance, mimic this theme in your landscape. Also try to use building materials that echo those used inside the house. If your kitchen uses slate floor tiles, for example, an adjoining outdoor patio can use similar paving to create a sense of unity. Designing in this way will make your landscape seem like a natural extension of your home when you look out upon it from the indoors.

• Build your landscape using trees, plants, and other materials that you see in other nearby yards. If your neighborhood is filled with stately oaks, filling your yard with birch trees will make it look rather unnatural. Taking your design ideas from those used successfully by your neighbors can also make your landscape seem larger and more majestic. Neighbors planning their landscapes together can create a truly wonderful effect.

Choosing familiar plants also has a practical benefit: if they are growing well in your neighbors' landscapes, you can be fairly certain these plants will thrive in the conditions found in your yard.

A neighborhood in which several landscapes feature similar trees, flowers, and building materials has a wonderfully unified atmosphere. Everyone benefits when neighbors design their landscapes in cooperation with one another.

Consider the topography and natural history of your region and neighborhood when designing your landscape. The style of this home and landscape is perfectly suited to the mountainous, forested region in which it is located.

Balance

The term *balance* is often used to describe the proper proportioning of visual "weight" in a landscape. In a perfectly balanced landscape, all the elements are arranged symmetrically. Symmetrical balance is appropriate for certain formal landscape styles, but in most instances it's best to seek an asymmetrical balance, in which the overall visual weight is roughly balanced, but without perfect symmetry. For example, if your house forms a large visual mass at one side of your yard, you can balance it by positioning a large shade tree (or a group of several smaller trees) on the other side of the yard.

Even a small space can balance many different family activities.

A well-planned outdoor home also is balanced in function. Areas designed for active family life should be balanced with one or two quiet areas where an individual can retreat in privacy. Spaces designed for kids should be offset by spaces planned with adult needs in mind. An outdoor home needs areas dedicated to pure visual appeal, but it also needs areas devoted to practical functions, such as storage and maintenance.

The concept of *scale* is closely related to that of balance. Scale refers to the relative size of elements within a landscape. In a balanced landscape, the scale of the various elements is consistent and logical. A very large yard calls for large trees, wide paths, and spacious areas of lawn. In a very small yard, on the other hand, dwarf tree species and potted plants might be more appropriate.

Regardless of the overall size of your landscape, elements that will normally be viewed at a distance should be larger or more coarsely textured, while small, fine-textured elements should be nearby, where they can be fully appreciated. In a border garden surrounding a patio, for example, position large, coarse shrubs and tall flowers with large blooms in the background, and place low plants with small blooms near the front of the garden.

The term *balance* usually describes visual weight in a landscape, but it can also describe a state of equilibrium between any pair of opposing principles, elements, or functions. Whenever one "look" threatens to dominate a landscape, it's a good idea to consider balancing it with an opposite to save your landscape from monotony. Balance large areas of subdued, monochromatic color by creating some spots of dramatic color. Strong horizontal lines, such as walkways and decks, can be countered with a vertical element, such as a fence, arbor, or row of columnar shrubs or trees.

OTHER EXAMPLES OF VISUAL BALANCE:
- **Coarse textures balanced by fine textures.** Lawn grass is a fine-textured surface that should be balanced by coarse-textured elements, such as a stepping-stone path or a broad-leafed tree or shrub.
- **Straight lines balanced by curved.** Most homes

Lawn grass is very fine-textured, and should be balanced with plants with larger leaves and a coarser texture. In this outdoor room, an edging of hosta provides this balance.

Your landscape should be balanced in terms of function. Include areas that appeal to all members of the family. This yard includes rooms dedicated to adults, as well as play areas for children.

and building sites are square and have straight edges. Designing curved pathways or planting areas with sweeping edges can do much to balance the landscape and save it from monotony.

This apple tree trained against a fence (a technique called espalier) *shows how vertical lines can be balanced by horizontal lines.*

- **Conformity balanced by surprise.** A landscape that is otherwise relentless in its uniformity can be brought to life by including one or two surprising focal points. A formal, symmetrical Colonial landscape, for instance, becomes more interesting if it includes a single piece of strikingly modern sculpture.
- **Softscape balanced by hardscape.** Too much of anything is bad—in your outdoor home as in any aspect of life. A landscape should be a balance of living plants (softscape) and structural building materials, such as wood, stone, and brick (hardscape). Good landscape designers suggest that hardscape flooring surfaces make up about half of your landscape, with the rest carpeted with lawn grass or other plants. A yard with nothing but plants looks wild and incomplete; a landscape consisting of nothing but brick, wood, and stone looks sterile and lifeless.

A small, unusual piece of statuary can provide balance to an otherwise traditional garden.

Movement

The concept of *movement* is critical to an outdoor home, both for practical and aesthetic reasons. The idea of movement has more implications than you might first realize.

PHYSICAL MOVEMENT

Like the inside of your house, an outdoor home must provide the means for people to move between the different spaces. Just as a house includes hallways, doors, and stairs, a landscape uses sidewalks, driveways, garden steps, and gates to control movement. Proper placement of these traffic paths is just as important outdoors as it is indoors. Well-planned gates and walkways provide easy access to the different living areas, while directing traffic efficiently. On a kitchen deck used for outdoor meals, for instance, it's best to position the deck stairs so the natural path from the door of the house to the yard doesn't conflict with the dining space.

Consider the purpose of each outdoor room when planning the position, layout, and materials for the physical pathways. For example, in a utility area running from a side entrance to the garbage collection area, a basic concrete sidewalk running in a straight line is most practical. In a room devoted to ornamental gardening, on the other hand, it might be better to create a meandering stepping-stone path that carries the visitor on a leisurely tour of the landscape's most interesting features.

VISUAL MOVEMENT

In landscapes, a sense of visual or symbolic movement is just as important as physical movement. Unlike the interior of your house, the outdoor home is a dynamic space with many elements that constantly change—from morning to night, from season to season, and from year to year. For this reason, it's

This landscape incorporates several types of literal and figurative movement. Pathways and stairs lead people between the outdoor rooms. Visual movement is implied by the archway and in the angles of the retaining wall timbers.

important that your landscape be designed so there are strong, continuous visual lines—pathways that lead the eye and intrigue the mind.

Visual pathways can be created in a number of ways. Mulched planting areas that extend around the entire outdoor home can gently lead the eye around the landscape and provide a sense of unity. Shrubs and flowers repeated throughout the landscape can also lend a sense of visual movement. A floor of lawn grass that occasionally narrows to form pathways between different outdoor spaces also serves this important function.

Don't forget vertical space when planning for visual movement. Because most of the visual lines in a landscape are horizontal, a few well-planned vertical elements can help provide contrast and interest. Picket fences, ornamental flowers with a tall growth habit, and columnar-shaped trees and shrubs can all provide vertical movement in a landscape.

TIME

Another type of movement to consider when planning your outdoor home is the passage of time. Think carefully about how the function and look of your landscape will change as morning moves into afternoon, as summer moves into fall and winter, as this year gives way to the future. The sun's position in the sky will change over the course of each day and over the passage of the seasons, which can have a clear impact on how you use your landscape. The deck you use for sunbathing on June afternoons, for example, may receive no sun at all in September. The trees and many other softscape materials you plant this year will grow steadily larger, which can dramatically change the look of your landscape, and sometimes even its function. Within a decade, a row of "shrubs" planted as a privacy screen may become overgrown shade trees that shed leaves into your swimming pool and block the sunlight needed to grow grass.

Also consider your personal time budget when planning your outdoor home. Do you enjoy yard work and welcome it as an enjoyable way to exercise and relax? Or do you prefer a low-maintenance landscape that frees you for other activities?

DECORATIVE MOVEMENT

Finally, elements that create literal motion can be an important source of visual interest in a landscape. Including a small fountain or circulating waterfall is one way to create interesting motion in your landscape. A colorful canvas awning, a wind sock, tall grasses, or a quaint whirligig that catches the wind can also provide this benefit.

In midsummer, a landscape will be at its most complex and colorful. Design simplicity is an important virtue at this time of year.

In autumn and winter, muted earth tones will dominate the landscape. Now, texture and shape become more prominent than color.

Interest

It's possible to create a landscape that doesn't quite succeed even though it dutifully applies all the design concepts discussed on the previous pages. A landscape can be unified, balanced, harmonious, simple, and perfectly suited to its purpose—but it can still be dull.

To create interest, design your landscape so each living space has some element chosen for its ability to draw the attention of the physical senses, the intellect, or the emotions.

SENSORY INTEREST

Elements that appeal to the bodily senses—sight, sound, touch, and smell—are very helpful for creating interest in a landscape.

Sight. Because sight tends to be the most dominant of the senses, the techniques for creating visual interest in a landscape receive much attention.

Strikingly colorful flowers in many contrasting hues provide the interest in this yard.

• Use contrasting colors, textures, and patterns. In a yard dominated by the fine texture and uniform color of lawn grass, for example, introducing some coarse-textured hardscape materials and bright flowering plants can make the landscape much more interesting to the eye.

• Create surprise in your landscape by introducing one or two unexpected features. In very formal, symmetrical landscapes, for instance, a colored, reflective gazing ball can add a touch of surprising abstraction. A great way to create the feeling of surprise and mystery is to lay out your landscape so that

The reflective gazing ball is a traditional accent piece currently enjoying a comeback.

some areas aren't immediately visible to the eye. A path that curves around a grove of trees and disappears into a hidden area is sure to draw visitors toward its mystery.

• Provide variety in your selection of building materials, plants, and accents. Many landscape accessories are designed for the sole purpose of lending visual interest to your yard. Landscape ponds, garden statues, trellises, and arbors are some accessories you might consider. Use them sparingly, though, because variety can very easily become clutter.

Sound. Though it receives less attention than sight, sound is very effective for creating interest in a landscape. A fountain or self-circulating waterfall adds the musical sound of cascading water to the outdoor home. Wind chimes and songbirds can also provide appealing sounds.

A water feature, such as a birdbath, creates interest in many ways. Water reflects sunlight, creating bright highlights in your landscape. The musical sound of running or splashing water appeals to the hearing. And water features draw birds and other wildlife to your landscape.

Many outdoor rooms feature a single accent piece to provide interest. Here, a decorative urn planted with flowers is the focal point of the landscape.

Smell and touch. Including a few fragrant flowers, trees, and shrubs in your landscape is a wonderful way to add interest. Be selective, though, because too many aromatic plants can be overwhelming. The sense of touch can be courted by clever use of building materials, especially in flooring surfaces. The texture of a stone or gravel walkway can be quite pleasant to the feet. Sunlight and wind also offer tactile appeal, and should be considered as you plan your landscape.

INTELLECTUAL INTEREST

A landscape can create interest by appealing to the mind. A well-chosen statue or pot can ignite the imagination and pique the intellect. Plant tags identifying the species of various flowers and shrubs can also stimulate thought. For an amateur naturalist, a landscape designed to welcome birds and animals can be greatly appealing. If you're among this group, you might want to include a birdbath and feeders, or a flower garden that will appeal to butterflies.

EMOTIONAL INTEREST

Elements chosen for their nostalgic or sentimental value create strong emotional interest in a landscape. Family keepsakes, such as an antique mailbox, garden tool, or planter, can be good accent pieces. A set of child's handprints can turn a plain concrete sidewalk or driveway into a fond reminder of family history. Plants, too, can create emotional interest— either for personal or historical reasons. In some families, treasured plants are handed down from generation to generation. Other plants seem to possess an inherent emotional appeal. Rose bushes, oak trees, crocuses, and daffodils are among the many plants that speak directly to our emotions.

A garden statue can be the perfect stimulus for emotional and intellectual interest in a landscape.

Concepts

Harmony

Harmony is achieved by making sure all the hardscape and softscape elements in your landscape complement one another. In short: the plants and building materials used in your outdoor home should all look good when viewed together.

The key to creating harmony in the outdoor home is to think carefully about how each element will relate to the overall landscape picture. Paving materials, walls and fences, furniture, plants, light fixtures, and decorations should all be chosen with an eye to the overall image of your landscape.

One way to develop a harmonious landscape is by starting with the big picture and gradually moving to the fine details.

REGIONAL HARMONY

Most modern communities feature a wide range of architectural styles, and the range of landscape styles is often just as broad. But it's likely there will be a few landscape styles that feel most natural in your region. It's helpful to look at natural landscapes for clues about how to create a landscape that is in harmony with your region. Designing your yard to resemble the natural habitats in your area is a good way to create harmony. If you live in a forested area, in other words, consider a woodland landscape. If you live in Nebraska, a prairie-style landscape is a natural fit. There are exceptions to every rule, but in general it's best to avoid a landscape style that sharply contrasts with the surrounding countryside. In an arid Southwest community, a yard planted with towering evergreens will not only be difficult to maintain, it also might look rather silly.

ARCHITECTURAL HARMONY

The next place to look for guidance in creating a harmonious landscape is your house. Look at the overall architecture of your home and the construction materials that were used to build it, and let this information guide your landscaping decisions. If your home is faced with natural flagstone, for example, a landscape that uses natural stone in its patios and walkways will look more harmonious than one that uses paver bricks. Basic construction style plays a part, too. A very formal, symmetrical landscape will clash badly if designed around a rustic, cottage-style home, while an informal, English-style landscape will look quite natural.

COLOR HARMONY

The term "harmony" sometimes has a different meaning among designers talking about the use of color, but we'll define harmonious colors as any group of colors that enhance or complement each other rather than clashing. Color harmony is a strong consideration for garden designers choosing plants, but it should also be considered when choosing colors for building materials and accessories.

The theory behind color harmony is complicated, involving the science of light wavelength and temperature, but there's really no reason to worry about the technical explanations. Using the classic color wheel—a graphic model that designers use to show the relationship of colors—designing a harmonious color scheme is quite simple.

In general, color harmony in the landscape is achieved by using hues that are either related or complementary, while avoiding color combinations that contrast or clash.

Related colors are those located adjacent to one another on the color wheel. Because these colors reflect areas of the light spectrum that are close together in wavelength, the eye and brain easily

The ultimate goal of any landscape is achieving harmony between the manmade and natural elements. In this outdoor room, the statue with its outspread arms is in perfect harmony with the soaring branches of the surrounding trees.

74

Choosing related colors creates a restful, reassuring look in the landscape. This garden features flowers in related shades of blue and purple.

and enhance one another: purples look brighter when contrasted with yellows, for example. Complementary color schemes are good for active, social areas of the outdoor home, such as a children's play

Contrasting colors, when used selectively, can create surprise and interest in a landscape. In this garden, pink foxgloves contrast sharply with the predominant yellows and oranges.

process the visual image. The effect is soothing and reassuring. For this reason, a design using related colors is ideal for quiet, private areas of the landscape. An outdoor room that features different shades of green and blue, for example, is likely to be a very restful environment.

Complementary colors are those that fall opposite one another on the color wheel. Complementary pairs exaggerate

area or recreational deck.

Contrasting colors are those that are neither related nor complementary. On the color wheel, contrasting colors have three colors between them. Contrasting colors often clash and are jarring to the eye, so it's generally best not to juxtapose them. Sometimes, however, contrasting colors can be used effectively to add surprise, drama, and interest in a landscape.

A landscape that makes good use of living things and natural materials is always harmonious.

Landscape Styles

Style in landscape design is a product of careful decision making. A sense of style is nothing more than the ability to choose the right building materials, plants, and furnishings, and arrange them in a way that creates a coherent "look" or theme. All it takes is patience, along with a basic understanding of practical design principles, which you learned in the last chapter. As you begin to make these important choices, it's helpful to keep the following ideas in mind:

Eclectic vs. Traditional: If you're adventurous, it's possible to create your own landscape style by choosing and arranging diverse elements in any fashion that pleases you, with little regard to tradition. Landscapes designed in this highly personal way are said to be *eclectic* in style, and they can be quite beautiful and unique. They can also be quite comical and bizarre. The success or failure of an eclectic landscape depends entirely on the taste and skill of you, the designer.

Another, perhaps safer, strategy is to model the look of your yard after one of several dozen traditional landscape styles (several of these are described on the following pages). Some landscape styles are modeled after historical periods, while others mimic different geographic looks. Following an accepted style makes it easier to achieve a look of harmony, but you should also make sure your landscape has at least a few personal touches.

Many great landscapes blend the traditional and eclectic approaches. Choose an overall style that fits the look of your home and the context of your neighborhood, but use materials, plants, and furnishings that have strong personal appeal to you.

Formal vs. Informal: Depending on your personality, you may prefer a very orderly, symmetrical landscape, or a more freewheeling, informal yard. If you have no strong personal preference, then you can let your house style guide your decision.

Formal landscapes often work best for homes that fit historical styles. A Colonial or French chateau-style home, for example, is a natural fit for a formal landscape. Formal landscapes make strong use of geometric shapes, and they have a strong central line (or axis) that creates a feeling of permanence. Formal styles tend to be symmetrically balanced, with shapes and lines that are mirrored from side to side.

Informal landscapes often work best for more modern homes. Informal styles use sweeping, curved lines and often include rolling lawns. They often include natural wooded areas and may include elements of surprise. Informal landscapes usually require less maintenance than formal landscapes, which may be an important consideration for you.

A Catalog of Traditional Styles

Colonial Style

Home style: This landscape style is best suited for a large yard and a large, two-story home finished in brick or lap siding. Homes that have an entryway with pillars or columns blend well with Colonial landscapes.

General layout: Colonial landscapes generally feature a formal main entry, often edged with symmetrical plantings of shrubs or flowers. The secondary entry and garage are frequently hidden. Driveways may be hidden behind shrubs to preserve large expanses of unbroken lawn, carefully edged and manicured. Planting areas are often rounded, featuring large, smooth curves.

Building materials: Flooring surfaces are often paver brick or natural stone. Garden walls may be constructed from brick or natural stone, and fences made from wood pickets or wrought iron are typical. Planting areas are often mulched with wood chips and edged with brick.

Plants: Large, deciduous shade trees indigenous to the region are common; oaks, sycamores, maples, and lindens are good choices. Boxwood hedges are often used, as are neatly trimmed deciduous shrubs.

Accessories & decorations: Themes of patriotism and heritage are common, including national flags and historical statuary.

Cottage Style

Home style: Smaller, bungalow-style homes built before 1950 are a natural match to this landscape style, although the look can be adapted to fit all but the most formal of architectural styles.

General layout: Much of the floor space in this landscape style is given over to ornamental plantings. Planting areas are often laid out and edged quite formally, but the plant arrangements within these beds are usually very diverse and informal. Grass meanders through the various outdoor rooms, serving more as a pathway material than as a traditional lawn. Even small landscapes make plentiful use of pathways, gates and archways. Many cottage landscapes include several quiet sitting areas, carefully positioned to provide spots for quiet reflection and relaxation.

Building materials: Natural stone or sand-set brick flooring surfaces are common in cottage landscapes. Garden walls normally use dry-fit natural stone. Fences are built from wooden pickets and are often painted white.

Plants: These landscapes often include small ornamental trees and flowering shrubs; climbing roses are another favorite feature. Flower gardens are plentiful and large, and tend to include older heritage or "heirloom" species, such as delphinium, foxglove, snapdragon, hollyhock, clematis, and English rose. To emphasize the cozy, miniature scale of the cottage architecture, the edges of the landscape are sometimes planted with very large trees that sharply contrast with the small house structure.

Accessories & decorations: Natural ponds, birdbaths, and light-hearted statuary of people or animals are regular features of cottage landscapes. Ornamental stone or metal lanterns are sometimes used. Wood furniture in classic English styles will complement this landscape.

Estate Style

Home style: Estate landscapes are best suited to large, formal-style homes situated on very spacious suburban sites. In the city, a two-story brick home set well back from the street can also support an estate style landscape. Architecture influenced by classic French or Italian influences often calls for this landscape treatment.

General layout: The overall landscape effect is one of formality and symmetry. The landscape strives to make the front entry the focal point, and circular drives looping past a formal entry are common. Lawn areas are carefully manicured and have perfectly rounded curves. Landscape elements are usually large and bold to match the scale of the home. Where space allows, an estate-style landscape can be framed with wooded areas.

Building materials: Paver brick driveways, walkways, and edgings are typical, though mortared natural stone is sometimes used. Landscape walls are often made of iron fencing or brick.

Plants: Large trees and shrubs are used to create shape and mass in the landscape and balance the weight of the house. Ornamental flower beds are often planted with bright bedding annuals arranged for bold geometric effect. Shaped hedges and shrubs are common features.

Accessories & decorations: Sizable fountains and statuary are often seen in this landscape style, as are large formal ponds. Large, decorative planting urns may be featured, and wrought-iron or teak furniture is popular. Driveways and walkways are often lined with landscape lighting.

COLONIAL

This traditional landscape shows many features of the Colonial style: symmetrical layout, deciduous hedges, and native shade trees. The driveway and garage are blocked by shade trees and large shrubs to preserve the balance of the front yard.

COTTAGE

In classic cottage landscape fashion, this yard includes a wide variety of colorful flowers and shrubs. The use of natural stone in the planting areas, and the painted picket fence and archway, are also typical in cottage landscapes.

ESTATE

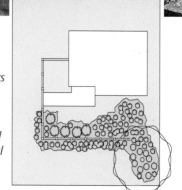

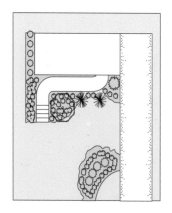

Estate-style landscapes are most appropriate for large, formal homes on expansive sites. Here, the sweeping curves of the lawn and planting areas are consistent with the estate style.

Ranch Style

Home style: Modern, one-story rambler-style homes are compatible with this landscape style.

General layout: The overall style of this landscape is simple and understated to be consistent with the uncomplicated architecture of the house. Overall, the lines of the landscape are low and horizontal, although one or two vertical elements may be included for contrast. A small courtyard or patio surrounding the front entry is a common feature. Foundation plantings are usually minimal.

Building materials: Wood fences may use split rails or horizontal boards to match the horizontal lines of the house. Poured concrete, paver brick, and wood decking are popular flooring choices and should be chosen to complement the materials used on the exterior of the house. Retaining walls are usually constructed from landscape timbers or rough-textured concrete block products.

Plants: Low-spreading shrubs and trees are the most commonly used plants. Ornamental flowers are used with restraint, and are often limited to low-maintenance species.

Accessories & decorations: Pioneer or western themes are often used, as shown by the popularity of brick barbecues and stone fire pits. Flowers in pots or hanging baskets are common.

Natural Woodland

Home style: Rustic-style homes and modern split-levels can both be appropriate for a woodland landscape. Houses with stained or natural wood siding lend themselves well to this style.

General layout: Woodland landscapes are decidedly informal in look. Lawn areas typically mimic the appearance of a woodland meadow, with soft meandering borders that gradually give way to shrubs and shade trees. Lawns are often inset with islands of ornamental shrubs and flowers in natural-looking arrangements.

Building materials: Natural stone and wood decking are the most commonly used flooring surfaces. Where a solid wall is needed, unpainted wood fencing is the most common choice, but rubblestone garden walls are also used.

Plants: Towering trees, both deciduous and evergreen, are common features of this landscape style. Softscape flooring choices often include ground cover other than grass, especially in shady areas. Boundaries between outdoor rooms are often formed with ornamental shrubs chosen for their wild, exuberant look. Flower beds are large and diverse, and are often planted with wildflowers or related hybrid species. Herb and vegetables are also common.

Accessories & decorations: Birdbaths, animal feeders, rustic benches, and adirondack chairs are traditional furnishings. A stone fire pit is a good addition.

Victorian

Home style: Large, two-story wood houses built near the turn of the century can readily accommodate this landscape style. Houses with porches, steep roofs, and painted "gingerbread" detailing are especially well suited to a Victorian landscape.

General layout: Victorian landscapes are usually dramatic, to complement the boldness of the house architecture. But to avoid visual competition with the ornate trim and sharp angles of the house, the lines of this style usually follow smooth, simple curves.

Building materials: Painted wood is a favorite building material in Victorian landscapes, and fences, gazebos, and other structures often echo the same detailing and colors found in the house trim. Natural stone is another popular building material, and is often used for walkways.

Plants: The Victorian era was a period of intense botanical exploration, and a true Victorian landscape reflects this in a broad selection of colorful, old-fashioned perennial flowers. Large beds of massed annuals are also common, planted in colors that complement the house trim. Fragrant flowers planted near the porch can make it a delightful place to relax. Flowering shrubs, especially rhododendrons and azaleas, are popular in Victorian landscapes.

Plantings around the foundations are kept minimal, to avoid covering up the trim details and preserve the view from the porch, but one or two large trees placed out in the yard can help balance the visual weight of the house. Weeping trees, such as willow and some varieties of flowering crab, are traditional features of Victorian landscapes.

Accessories & decorations: Hanging pots of bright flowers often adorn the porches of Victorian homes. Classic wood or simple wrought-iron furniture is a good fit in these landscapes, and ornamental pots and statuary are frequently used as accents.

Water features, such as a large fountain in the front or a pond in the backyard, are often a part of this landscape style.

RANCH

WOODLAND

In this adaptation, low foundation plantings complement the low design of the house. Although the plant selection here is more diverse than is typical, the use of low-maintenance perennials is consistent with the style.

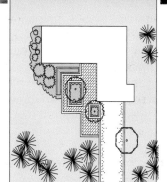

Woodland landscapes typically use towering trees and are quite informal and rustic in appearance. Wood and natural stone are favorite building materials, and ornamental plants are usually shade-tolerant species.

VICTORIAN

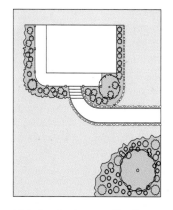

Victorian landscapes, like the one shown here, are colorful yet simple. The lines are smooth and curved, and old-fashioned plants predominate. Painted wood and natural stone are the most popular building materials in this landscape style. Hanging baskets and flowering shrubs are common decorative elements.

Contemporary Style

Home style: Modern architectural styles with strong angular lines lend themselves to this landscape type. Traditional ramblers and split-level homes can also be well-suited to a contemporary landscape style.

General layout: The overall effect of a contemporary landscape style is often abstract. Dramatic, free-flowing lines predominate in these landscapes, a strategy that helps unify the yard with the architecture of the house. Extensive foundation plantings are typical. Planting areas tend have bold geometric or rounded shapes, and are used with hardscape edgings. Long, wide walkways are often included, styled to boldly lead the eye to the main entry.

Building materials: Paver brick, wood decking, and poured concrete are typical flooring choices. Retaining walls are usually built from wood timbers or textured concrete block chosen to complement the building materials used in the house. Fences are usually constructed with natural wood and vertical picket styling.

Plants: Shrubs, ground covers, and small flowering trees are used extensively; ornamental flowers are used with restraint. Low-maintenance plants are typical in these landscapes. Shade trees with striking bark or attractive textures are popular; choices include pine, birch, honey-locust, mountain ash, ginko, and palm. Weeping trees are also popular. A small flowering tree is often included for accent.

Accessories & decorations: Modern, contemporary furnishings and accents are appropriate, since older, traditional styles usually look out of place. Abstract fountains and statuary can be used to good effect. Landscape lighting with dramatic uplighting effects is common.

Country Farm Style

Home style: Large, two-story homes with traditional, painted lap siding work best for this landscape style. Homes with open porches—especially wrap-around porches—are well suited for country farm landscapes.

General layout: The overall effect in a country farm landscape is informal and down-to-earth. Large landscape elements, such as large trees, vegetable gardens, and flower beds, are usually included in order to balance the visual weight of the home. Lawn areas tend to meander through the outdoor rooms, mimicking the look of a flowing meadow, and may be interrupted with large island planting areas. Lawn areas gradually give way to border areas planted with prairie flowers and grasses, or with woodland shrubs and trees. Foundation plantings are usually rather narrow and restrained.

Building materials: Wood and natural stone predominate in paved floor areas and for walls. Natural split-rail fences are common in backyard areas, while painted fences with horizontal rails are popular in front yards.

Plants: Fruit trees, vegetables, and herbs are more common here than in most other landscape styles. Shade trees are large to balance the weight of the house. Columnar trees are sometimes planted in rows bordering the edge of the yard to mimic the look of a farm windbreak. Flowers tend to be heritage varieties, such as foxglove, delphinium, snapdragon, and hollyhock.

Accessories & decorations: Rural, rustic themes are popular. Antique farm implements are common decorations, as are wooden mailboxes, yard signs, and weather vanes.

Mediterranean Style

Home style: Italian, Spanish, Mexican, and southern California architectural styles lend themselves to this type of landscape. Many one-story stucco homes are a natural fit for Mediterranean-style landscapes.

General layout: Mediterranean landscapes with Italian and Spanish influence are often multilevel, though California and Southwest variations are often flat. The entry area is often given over to a courtyard or large patio, and there may be several paved patio areas in the landscape.

Building materials: Textured concrete and geometric paver bricks are popular for paved flooring areas. Brick or stucco garden walls are often used in this landscape style, as is wrought-iron fencing.

Plants: Species that tolerate dry conditions are best suited to this landscape. Low-maintenance ground covers are often used instead of grass in lawn areas. Small fruit trees, such as citrus or olive, are common features, and small shade trees are sometimes inset into patios. Bright annual flowers planted in large pots add spots of color to the landscape.

Accessories & decorations: Terra-cotta planters are popular features, and stone benches are also common. Spanish and Italian styles can make extensive use of statuary, ornamental urns, and water features, such as fountains and formal pools. Landscape lighting is a common feature, and it often includes uplighting of trees and other elements.

CONTEMPORARY

This modern home uses several elements typical in contemporary landscapes: low shrubs, extensive foundation plantings, and small specimen trees with attractive bark. Most contemporary landscapes are conservative and restrained in their use of color.

COUNTRY FARM

In a country farm home, the landscape generally uses large masses to balance the weight of the house. Here, extensive foundation plantings help the house blend into the landscape, but the shrubs are kept low to preserve an open view from the porch.

MEDITERRANEAN

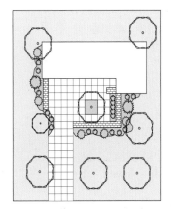

Like most Mediterranean landscapes, this California-style home makes extensive use of brick and stone paving. The entry courtyard, with its potted plants and spacious, spreading shade tree, is also typical of this landscape style.

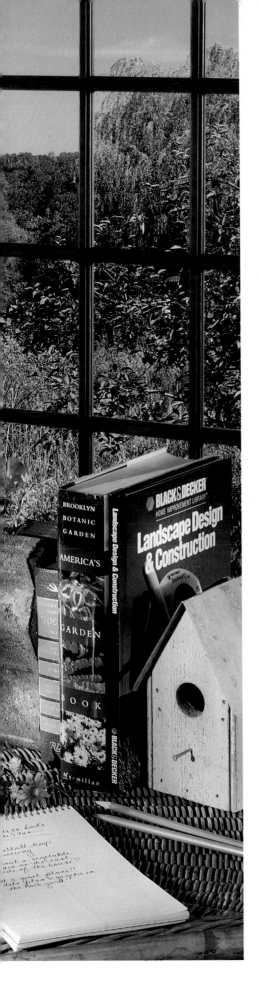

Making Plans

Now that you've learned a bit about the basics of landscape design, you're ready to start the hands-on process of creating working plans for your new outdoor home. The best way to do this is by working through the following chapters in order. Refer back to the Basics section for help if you find yourself stalled at any point. By the time you finish the book, you'll have a complete plan package for building your new landscape, including a full-color final design, working plans with all specifications, a demolition plan, and planting maps.

It pays to take your time with this process. A leisurely approach to planning yields better results than rushing the work. Many professional landscape designers tell their clients to spend a full year thinking about and refining their landscape plans before the hands-on construction work begins. At the very least, we think it's a good idea to spend several weeks—or even months—to develop a plan. This may seem like a long time, but you'll probably find that it passes very quickly, since the process is a lot of fun. Planning your yard is a great way to spend free time when you can't be outdoors. During cold winter months or on rainy afternoons, what could be better than dreaming about your new landscape?

IN THIS SECTION

Gathering Information . . . . page 86
Drawing Plans . . . . page 98

Gathering Information

IN THIS CHAPTER

Brainstorming .... page 88
Budgeting .... page 90
Courtesies & Codes .... page 92
The Yard Survey .... page 96

Now that you have an understanding of the landscape elements and the principles of design, you're ready to begin creating an actual plan for your new landscape. The first step in this process is to develop a foundation of facts and ideas.

Some of the most important information will come from looking at the needs and opinions of you and your family. Unless your landscape is designed with all users in mind, it won't succeed completely, so make sure everyone in the family is considered. A landscape with elaborate flower beds and many shrubs might please you, but it may disappoint your teenager, who was hoping for a basketball court. You might love the look of a huge green lawn, but it might not look so great to the family member who must mow it each week.

Some people have no trouble visualizing a new landscape and expressing their tastes. But if you have difficulty with this, there are many sources of information that can stimulate ideas. Magazines, books, and television programs can help crystallize your opinions, and visits to public gardens and arboretums can be especially useful.

As you plan your outdoor home over the next few weeks, carry a camera with you. Take snapshots of private yards and public landscapes that appeal to you. Stop and talk to homeowners whose yards catch your eye. Avid do-it-yourself gardeners and landscapers almost always enjoy sharing their ideas.

You'll need to determine an appropriate budget for your landscape. Planning can't proceed unless you have a realistic idea of how much a landscape should cost—and how much you can afford to spend.

Creating a great landscape will also depend on how well you know your own yard and understand its relationship to the surrounding neighborhood and community. Careful observation and measurement of physical dimensions, sun and shadow patterns, and other details will be crucial to your landscaping plans. A good plan also takes into consideration the appearance of surrounding properties and the opinions of your neighbors. Your community government may also have something to contribute to your landscaping plans, in the form of local Building Codes. These regulations provide guidelines for creating a safe landscape that meets community standards.

Many landscaping materials are available free of charge. For example, your community may have a wood chip pile or compost site where you can obtain mulch. Stone for landscaping can sometimes be scavenged from building sites. Demolition sites can provide second-hand brick and concrete rubble.

Budgeting

Before you begin to dream in earnest, it's a good idea to figure out how much you can (or should) spend on your outdoor home. It's easy to get discouraged at this stage, but don't let the dollar amounts scare you off. In fact, you can probably afford more landscape than you first think.

All-new landscapes. Professional landscape designers and real estate professionals say that it's reasonable to spend 10% to 15% of the total home value on professionally installed, all-new landscape, whether it's a first-time landscape for a newly constructed home or a complete demolition and reconstruction of an established yard.

If you do the work yourself, however, the total cost of an all-new landscape will be closer to 5% to 10% of your home's value. On a $200,000 home, this means you can expect to pay $10,000 to $20,000 for an all-new, do-it-yourself landscape.

Remodeled landscapes. Your costs may be considerably less if you're planning a "remodeled" landscape that will preserve some of the features of your present yard. When you do the installation yourself, it's possible to do a fairly extensive landscape renovation while spending 3% to 5% of your home's market value—$6,000 to $10,000 on our hypothetical $200,000 home.

Even this amount can seem like a very large sum, but there are many creative ways to make your landscape more affordable.

BORROWING

Like any home improvement, a landscape project can be funded with a home improvement loan or second mortgage. Or, you can refinance your principal mortgage to provide the money needed to remodel your outdoor home. Any interest you pay on a home improvement loan or mortgage will be tax deductible. There are other types of loans you can use to pay for a landscaping project, but in most cases the interest rates are higher, and the interest can't be deducted. A loan officer at your bank or credit union can explain the tax implications of any loan you want to consider.

PAYING OUT-OF-POCKET

Unlike most home improvements, a landscape can be renovated over a period of several years. Once you have a complete landscape plan, for instance, you might choose to complete just one outdoor room each year. Spending $1,000 to $2,000 annually, you can gradually build your landscape. You'll also save a considerable amount of money over the long run, since you won't be paying interest on borrowed money. If you choose to use this strategy, you may want to develop separate budgets for each room of your outdoor home.

CUTTING COSTS

Sales. It's possible to trim thousands of dollars off the cost of your landscape by shopping creatively. Like any retail business, building supply centers and landscape suppliers hold sales from time to time. In areas where landscaping is a seasonal business, look for bargains during the off-season months when retailers are trying to reduce inventory.

Discounted plants. Plants are often cheaper when purchased very early or very late in the growing season. In early spring, nurseries often hold special sales to draw in customers and, in the late fall they often close out inventory by holding big sales. Make

sure, however, that you don't buy diseased plants when you shop sales. If you're not ready to plant immediately, perennials and shrubs can be temporarily planted right in the pot until your landscape is ready for them.

Salvaging. With a little ingenuity, it's possible to obtain some building materials at no cost whatsoever. You can sometimes find fieldstone and other rock to use in retaining walls and other projects by scouting new-home construction sites. At demolition sites, you may be able to find brick that you can use in garden walls and pathways. Concrete rubble can be used to build retaining walls. If you see neighbors demolishing a fence or deck, ask if you can salvage the wood to use for planters or walkways.

Naturally, you should get permission from the owner or construction foreman before you collect building materials from any location.

Combining resources. Consulting with your neighbors might reveal ways to save costs. If your neighbors are also interested in doing some landscaping work, you might be able to buy large quantities of materials together to save money. Or perhaps you've got your heart set on a mortared stone wall but can't quite afford it. If your neighbor shares your enthusiasm, you might work out a plan to share the expense, since the wall will benefit both properties.

As you develop your landscape plan over the next chapters, keep notes on the costs of the building materials and accessories you are considering for each room of your outdoor home. Estimate the totals every so often to make sure you're not exceeding the overall budget you've set. The design process is about decision making. At times, you'll be forced to economize on some elements of your landscape in order to afford the elements that are most important to you.

TERM OF LOAN IN YEARS

Interest Rate	3	5	7	10
8.00%	31.34	20.28	15.59	12.13
8.25%	31.45	20.39	15.71	12.26
8.5%	31.56	20.51	15.83	12.39
8.75%	31.68	20.63	15.96	12.53
9.00%	31.79	20.75	16.08	12.66
9.25%	31.91	20.87	16.21	12.80
9.5%	32.03	21.00	16.34	12.93
9.75%	32.14	21.12	16.47	13.07
10.00%	32.27	21.28	16.60	13.22
10.25%	32.38	21.37	16.73	13.35
10.5%	32.50	21.49	16.86	13.49
10.75%	32.62	21.62	16.99	13.63
11.00%	32.73	21.74	17.12	13.77
11.25%	32.85	21.86	17.25	13.91
11.5%	32.97	21.99	17.38	14.05
11.75%	33.09	22.11	17.51	14.20
12.00%	33.21	22.24	17.65	14.34

This table shows you the monthly payments on a loan. To calculate your payments, you'll need to find the interest rate and the payback term of the loan, then find the corresponding index number in the chart. When you multiply this index number times the amount of your loan, in thousands, you'll discover what your monthly payments will be. Let's imagine that you're borrowing $10,000 at 10% interest, and you'll be paying it off over 5 years. Your monthly payment would be $212.80.

Courtesies & Codes

In principle, we'd like to tell you that you're free to design your landscape however you see fit. In practice, however, it's not quite that simple.

Unless you live in a rural area or on a farm, there probably are local regulations you'll need to consider when planning your outdoor home. Building Codes often restrict the height of fences or garden walls. Some of these rules are designed to protect public safety, while other are intended to preserve certain aesthetic standards. For instance, some communities prohibit "prairie-style" landscapes with tall grasses that contrast sharply with the neighborhood norm of carefully mown lawns.

In addition, and perhaps more importantly, you should also consider the feelings and opinions of your neighbors when planning your landscape, since changes to your own yard often affect them, as well. The tall hedge you plant for privacy, for example, might cast dense shade over your neighbor's sunbathing deck. Though such legal cases are rare, disagreements over landscaping have escalated into court battles.

Good manners dictate that you should at least discuss your plans with your neighbors to avoid hard feelings. And you may find that this courtesy reaps unexpected rewards. For instance, you and your neighbor might decide to share the labor and expense by landscaping both your properties at the same time. You could also save money by buying materials in bulk and sharing the delivery charges. Or you might combine your resources on a key feature that benefits both yards—such as a stone garden wall or shade tree. When several neighbors put their heads together to create an integrated landscape plan for their yards, the results benefit everyone. Individual landscapes look larger when the surrounding yards share a complementary look and style.

Finally, you should check with your local utility companies to pinpoint the locations of any underground electrical, plumbing, sewer, or telephone lines on your property. The locations of these features can have obvious importance if your landscape plans require digging or changes to the grade of the property. It costs nothing to have the utility companies identify the locations of these lines, and it can keep you from making an expensive and potentially life-threatening mistake.

On the following pages, you'll find some common legal restrictions for typical landscape projects.

FENCES

Good fences are said to make good neighbors, but in truth, few landscaping projects are more likely to offend a neighbor than a tall fence that suddenly interrupts a view they've grown to expect. If you consult them regarding no other feature, make sure to talk to your neighbors about any plans you have for a new fence or garden wall.

• **Height:** The maximum height of a fence may be restricted by your local Building Code. In some communities, backyard fences are limited to 6 ft. in height, while front yard fences are limited to 3 or 4 ft., or may be prohibited altogether.

• **Setback:** Even if not specified by your Building Code, it's a good idea to position your fence a foot or so inside the official property line to avoid any possible boundary disputes. Similarly, don't assume that the fence marks the exact boundary of your property. Before digging an elaborate planting bed up to the edge of your neighbor's fence, for example, it's best to make sure you're not encroaching on someone else's land.

• **Gates:** Gates must be at least 3 ft. wide—4 ft. if you plan on pushing a wheelbarrow through them.

DRIVEWAYS

• **Width:** Straight driveways should be at least 10 ft wide; 12 ft. is better. On sharp curves, the driveway should be 14 ft. wide.

• **Thickness:** Concrete driveways should be at least 6" thick.

• **Base:** Because it must tolerate considerable weight, a concrete or brick paver driveway should have a compactible gravel base that is at least 6" thick.

• **Drainage:** A driveway should slope $\frac{1}{4}$" per foot away from a house or garage. The center of the driveway should be crowned so it is 1" higher in the center than on the sides.

• **Reinforcement:** Your local Building Code probably requires that all concrete driveways be reinforced with iron rebar or steel mesh for strength.

SIDEWALKS & PATHS

• **Width of sidewalks:** Traditional concrete sidewalks should be 4 ft. to 5 ft. wide to allow two people to comfortably pass one another.

• **Width of garden paths:** Informal pathways may be 2 ft. to 3 ft. wide, although stepping-stone pathways can be even narrower.

• **Thickness of slab:** A poured concrete sidewalk should be 3" to 4" thick.

• **Base:** Most Building Codes require that a concrete or brick sidewalk be laid on a base of compactible gravel at least 4" thick.

• **Reinforcement:** Your local Building Code may require that standard concrete sidewalks be reinforced with iron rebar or steel mesh for strength.

• **Surface:** Concrete sidewalks should be textured to provide a nonslip surface.

• **Drainage:** Concrete sidewalks should be crowned or slanted $\frac{1}{4}$" per foot to ensure that water doesn't puddle on the surface.

• **Sand-set paver walkways:** Brick paver walkways should be laid on a 3"-thick base of coarse sand.

STEPS

• **Proportion of riser to tread depth:** The relationship between step rise and depth (run) is important. In general, steps should be proportioned so that the sum of the depth, plus the riser multiplied by two, is between 25" and 27". A 15" depth and 6" rise, for example, is a comfortable step (15 + 12 = 27); as is an 18" depth and 4" rise (18 + 8 = 26).

• **Railings:** Building Codes may require railings for any stairway with more than three steps, especially for stairs that lead to an entrance to your home.

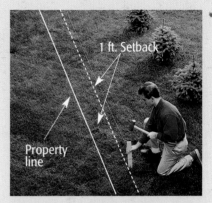

Fences should be set back at least 1 ft. from the formal property lines.

Driveways should be at least 10 ft. wide to accommodate vehicles.

Concrete paving should be laid on a bed of gravel to provide drainage.

Concrete steps should use a comfortable tread depth and riser height.

Information

CONCRETE PATIOS

• **Base:** Concrete patios should have a subbase layer of compactible gravel at least 4" thick.

• **Thickness:** Concrete slabs for patios should be at least 3" thick.

• **Reinforcement:** Concrete slabs should be reinforced with wire mesh or a grid of rebar.

GARDEN WALLS

• **Footings:** In many communities, mortared brick or stone garden walls more than 4 ft. in height require poured concrete footings that extend below the maximum winter frost line. Failure to follow this regulation can result in a hefty fine or a demolition order, as well as a flimsy, dangerous wall.

• **Drainage:** Dry-set stone garden walls installed without concrete footings should have a base of compactible gravel at least 6" thick to ensure the stability of the wall.

SWIMMING POOLS

• **Fences:** Nearly all Building Codes require a protective fence around swimming pools to keep young children and animals away from the water.

• **Location:** In some areas, Building Codes require that below-ground swimming pools be no closer than 10 ft. from a building foundation.

LIGHTING

• **Courtesy:** Neighbors may have a legitimate complaint if you install floodlights that shine onto their properties, so consider this when planning your lighting installation. Consulting neighbors during planning is a good way to prevent disagreements of this type. Choose neighbor-friendly fixtures with heads that limit the glare.

• **Safety:** Switches for landscape lighting fixtures may be no closer than 10 ft. from a pool, hot tub, fountain, or other water feature. In addition, many local Building Codes require that all outdoor circuits be protected by ground-fault circuit-interrupters (GFCIs).

FLOWERS

Neighbors and your local government may have something to say about the most basic of landscape elements—ornamental flowers.

Codes: Local ordinances and state law may prohibit the use of some flower species, especially those invasive species that threaten natural plant life.

Courtesy: Some flowers, such as violets, have such an aggressive growth habit that they can take over a lawn—both yours and, more importantly, your neighbor's. It's also possible that a neighbor might be allergic to some plants. Highly scented shrubs, such as lilacs, may be so unbearable to some people that it ruins their enjoyment of the outdoors. Planting your garden with bright flowers that draw bees will not be appreciated by a neighbor who is allergic to bee stings.

Safety: A surprisingly large number of plants contain toxins that can be poisonous if ingested. If small children will be playing in your yard, make sure to avoid such plants. Foxglove, monkshood, English ivy, nightshade, castor bean, and mistletoe are some of the common plants that pose some danger to small children.

TREES

• **Courtesy:** Consult your neighbors, especially if you're planning to plant one or more large trees in your yard. Trees cast shade, shed leaves and drop debris, and your neighbor will feel the impact of these events. Most neighbors welcome an attractive new shade tree, but check this out before finalizing your plans.

Concrete patios require reinforcement with steel mesh or rebar.

Frost line

Mortared garden walls need to be supported by concrete footings.

A pool requires a protective fence to keep neighborhood children and animals from falling in.

Codes: Certain tree species may be restricted by your community. In areas ravaged by Dutch elm or oak wilt disease, for example, these tree species may be prohibited.

• **Planting locations:** Regulations may restrict where you can plant trees. For example, boulevard areas that you routinely mow and care for actually belong to the city, which may determine what you plant in these areas. Local Building Code may also prohibit planting trees and shrubs near sewer lines or water mains.

• **Safety:** Your community has the power to force you to trim or remove large shade trees that pose a hazard or inconvenience. So, it makes practical sense to plant trees that are likely to experience good health and slow growth. Resist the temptation to plant fast-growing trees for quick shade. Within ten years or so, you'll be faced with cutting down trees that have rampantly taken over your landscape. Slow-growing species are much stronger and durable than fast growers, and they generally are more attractive, as well.

RETAINING WALLS

• **Height:** For do-it-yourself construction, retaining walls should be no more than 4 ft. high. Higher slopes should be terraced with two or more short retaining walls.

• **Batter:** A retaining wall should have a backward slant (batter) of 2" to 3" for dry-set stones; 1" to 2" for mortared stones.

• **Footings:** Retaining walls higher than 4 ft. must have concrete footings that extend down below the frost line. This helps ensure the stability of the wall.

PONDS

• **Safety:** To ensure the safety of children, some communities restrict landscape ponds to a depth of 12" or 18" unless surrounded by a protective fence or covered with heavy wire mesh.

DECKS

• **Structural members:** Determining the proper spacing and size for structural elements of a deck can be a complicated process, but if you follow these guidelines, you will satisfy Code requirements in most areas:

BEAM SIZE & SPAN

Beam size	Maximum spacing between posts
two 2 × 8s	8 ft.
two 2 × 10s	10 ft.
two 2 × 12s	12 ft.

JOIST SIZE & SPAN

Joist size	Maximum distance between beams (Joists 16" apart)
2 × 6	8 ft.
2 × 8	10 ft.
2 × 10	13 ft.

• **Decking boards:** Surface decking boards should be spaced so the gaps between boards are no more than 1/4" wide.

• **Railings:** Any deck more than 30" high requires a railing. Gaps between rails or balusters should be no more than 4".

• **Post footings:** Concrete footings should be at least 8" in diameter. If a deck is attached to a permanent structure, the footings must extend below the frost line in your region.

Slopes are best handled by installing a series of short retaining walls rather than one tall wall.

Building Codes require that railing balusters be spaced no more than 4" apart to keep small children from slipping through or being trapped between them.

Drawing Plans

IN THIS CHAPTER

Creating a Site Map .... page 100
Sketching Bubble Plans .... page 102
Drafting a Final Design .... page 104
Drawing Elevations .... page 106
Landscape Symbols .... page 107
Creating Working Plans .... page 108

Equipped with a strong sense of your needs and preferences, and supported by a clear understanding of your site, you're now ready to start drawing up detailed landscape plans.

Good landscape plans make it possible to determine your final budget and develop a practical schedule for completing the work. If you plan to build the landscape yourself, the plans will help you organize your work efficiently; if you intend to hire contractors to do some or all of the work, landscape plans will make it possible for them to give you accurate bids on the work.

Your final landscape plans will include several different scale drawings, each showing a different aspect: a *site map* that establishes the position of all elements in the existing site; a *bubble plan* that indicates how the new living spaces will be laid out on your site; a *final design* that shows all the features of the new landscape, illustrated in color; a *demolition plan* that shows the elements that will be removed; and *working plans* that indicate measurements and provide other information that will be needed for the actual construction process.

At each stage in the design process, you may find it useful to create elevation drawings that show important elements of the landscape from a side view. There's no need to draw elevations representing every part of your yard; but wherever your landscape has vertical elements or includes a significant slope, an elevation drawing will be helpful.

It's best to approach this important part of the planning process with a sense of adventure—the best landscape plans are the result of playful exploration and fearless trial and error. Take your time, experiment with many different layouts, and don't be afraid to make mistakes. A plan drawing is only paper, after all, and can easily be changed.

Sketching Bubble Plans

A bubble plan is a rough sketch that divides your yard into the outdoor rooms you expect to include in the finished landscape. Some designers call these drawings *zone plans*. Drawing bubble plans is actually a test-phase—a chance to really stretch your imagination and have fun with the design process.

Draw several variations of your ideas, and include some suggestions that seem a little extreme. Sometimes taking an idea to extremes leads you to see entirely new possibilities that can then be adapted into more realistic versions. Even experienced professional designers may go through as many as a dozen bubble plans before settling on a favorite. To save time as you experiment with different layouts, you can sketch on photocopies of a tracing of your site map.

Once you have several promising bubble plans, invite the other members of your household to review the layouts and give their opinions. Agreeing on the layout for your outdoor home can prevent disappointments later on and can encourage family members to help during the construction process. Your reluctant teenager might be coaxed into helping dig garden beds if he or she knows it will reduce lawn-mowing chores.

Step A: Trace the Site Map & Make Photocopies
1. Tape a sheet of tracing paper over your site map. (If you have trouble seeing the map through the paper, try taping the sheets to a window to make the lines more visible.)
2. Mark the corner points of all the structures and features that will be retained in your new landscape. Don't trace elements you plan to remove or demolish.
3. Use a drafting triangle to outline the buildings and other structures, using a black pen.
4. When the tracing is complete, trace or photocopy it. You may need a dozen or more copies as you experiment with potential layouts.

Step B: Sketch Potential Layouts
1. Using a copy of your tracing, draw a loose pencil sketch, laying out the various rooms of your landscape. Wherever possible, draw smooth, curved lines to represent the boundaries of each space, using a curve template as a guide. Make sure you give adequate space for each outdoor room. A 10 × 10 area is

TOOLS & MATERIALS

- Site map (page 100)
- Drafting triangle
- Tracing paper
- Pencil
- Curve template
- Ruler
- Stakes
- String
- Cardboard

A: *Make a tracing of your site map that includes the property boundaries and any structures and features that will be included in your new landscape.*

B: *Experiment with layouts for your landscape by drawing several different bubble plans. Use smooth, flowing lines for the boundaries of each living space.*

the minimum that should be allowed for any room other than a utility space. Don't worry yet about the precise edges for decks, patios, and other hardscape features that will form your landscape.

2. Experiment with several variations. As you draw, try to visualize how your landscape will look when viewed from the windows and doors of your house, from the street, and from your neighbors' yards.

Step C: Test the Bubble Plans

1. Evaluate the merits of each bubble plan in the real world—by laying out the room boundaries in your yard. Use a rope or a garden hose to outline the floor of each living space.

2. Use cardboard cutouts, or stakes and string, to represent the walls of your outdoor rooms, including fences, hedges, and garden walls. Pay particular attention to the flow of traffic patterns between rooms as you lay out the walls.

3. Outline the walkways and paths as indicated on the bubble plan, again using cardboard cutouts,

DESIGN TIP:

If you have original blueprints from the builder or landscape architect who worked on your house or yard, these can be used as the basis for your site map, bubble plans, and plan drawings. Trace or photocopy the blueprints and use the copies to make your bubble plans.

stakes and string, and rope or a garden hose. Walk along these proposed pathways and imagine the views that will be created.

4. Position lawn chairs, benches, and other accessories in the spaces to get a feel for how well the plan works for the activities you imagine will take place in the various rooms.

5. Walk around the living spaces, envisioning the completed rooms and making sure the traffic patterns are unobstructed. If your observations suggest changes, adjust the bubble plan as needed.

Step D: Choose the Best Bubble Plan

Now, choose the bubble plan layout that gives the best "feel" to you and your family. Label the various living spaces to indicate their purpose. This bubble plan will be the starting point as you turn to the following pages to begin drafting a final design.

C: Test different bubble plans in your yard by outlining the walls with rope or a hose, and by positioning cardboard cutouts to represent stepping-stones and walkways.

D: Select the bubble plan that best suits your needs and preferences. Redraw it carefully and label the various living spaces according to their purpose.

Drafting a Final Design

After choosing a bubble plan that gives the best rough layout for your new landscape, it's time to develop a final design drawing—a carefully drafted color rendition of your new landscape, based on your site map and selected bubble plan. This drawing will show all the elements of your outdoor home, represented by standard landscaping symbols (page 107) and illustrated in color. It will display the promise of your new landscape, and it will guide and inspire when you begin the actual construction process.

A final design drawing requires careful, detailed work. Expect some trial and error as you transform the rough layout represented by your bubble plan into a polished, professional-quality design drawing. Have several photocopies of your site map on hand, because you'll almost certainly have a false start or two before arriving at a final design.

One of the keys to a professional landscape design is to use smooth, flowing lines rather than straight lines and sharp angles. Strive to establish a continuous flow through all the rooms in your landscape. Unavoidable straight lines, such as property boundaries and city sidewalks, can be disguised with flowing planting beds that have curved borders. Shrubs, trees, and flower beds can also form internal boundaries between different spaces in your landscape. In your final design, the boundaries of each living space should resemble the flowing curves found in your bubble plan.

Also strive for a feeling of continuity between the various rooms of your outdoor home. Many people

TOOLS & MATERIALS

- Colored pencils
- Drafting pencil
- Ruler
- Circle template
- Curve template
- Symbols (pages 107 to 108)
- Site map photocopies

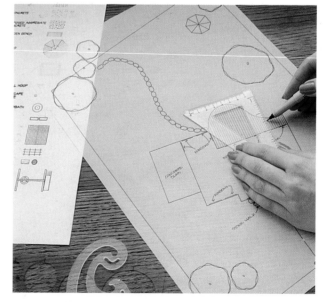

A: *Outline the hardscape flooring and ceiling structures on a fresh copy of the site map.*

use lawn grass as the unifying element. As it leaves one room, the lawn can narrow into a hallway passing through planting beds, then widen as it enters the next space. Repeated use of the same building materials or the same types of shrubs or flowers can also provide unity.

Step A: Draw in the Floors & Ceilings

1. On a fresh copy of your site map, outline any permanent hardscape flooring features you'll be installing, such as patios, decking, and walkways. Use your bubble plan for reference when positioning these elements, and use standard landscape symbols (page 107) to represent these structures.

2. Draw in any hardscape ceilings that will be included, such as awnings, pergolas, or gazebos.

3. Add any shade trees that will form softscape ceilings. Make sure to use outlines that approximate the *mature* sizes of all trees.

Step B: Add the Walls

1. Draw in any walls that will form the boundaries of outdoor rooms. Some will be physical barriers, such as fences, hedges, or garden walls, but other boundaries are simply implied by a sweeping row of low bushes or a planting area with gradual curves.

> **TIP:**
>
> If it's not practical for you to include full foundation plantings in your new landscape, concentrate on the corners of your house. Small beds of shrubs or flowers positioned at the corners of the house will do wonders for easing the transition into the outdoor home.

2. Make sure your boundaries include gaps or doors to direct traffic flow, and windows where you want to preserve or create an appealing view of the surrounding landscape.

3. Add detail to the transition areas, such as where the house meets the landscape, and where a sidewalk or driveway meets the lawn. Try to make these transitions soft and gradual, rather than abrupt. Where possible, soften fences and other straight walls by creating transitions that are smoothly curved. Planting beds are a good way to achieve subtle transitions.

4. Add in symbols and textures for all the remaining elements of your landscape, such as birdbaths, raised planting beds, landscape ponds, furnishings, and accents.

Step C: Finish the Design

1. Mark the locations of any permanent utility fixtures, such as landscape lights and hose spigots.

2. Use colored pencils to shade in the outlines for the various hardscape and softscape elements of your landscape plan. Start with the uppermost elements, such as tree canopies and arbors, and work down to the floors.

B: *Draw in the wall elements, including fences, garden walls, hedges, border gardens, and other planting areas. Also indicate gates and other "doors."*

C: *Add the symbols and textures for any remaining elements, then use colored pencils to finish the design.*

Drawing Elevations

Most drawings for a landscape plan are overhead "plan" or "map" views. These work fine for showing the overall layout of your landscape and the horizontal dimensions of its features. But for areas that have a vertical hardscape element, such as a fence, garden steps, elevated deck, arbor, or retaining wall, you'll also need an *elevation drawing*, which shows a side view of your planned landscape. Elevations are essential for estimating building materials and planning the construction of vertical elements.

It's not always necessary to draw the entire structure when making an elevation drawing. If you're planning a fence or garden wall on a flat yard, for example, you can draw the elevation for a small section representing the construction pattern that will be used throughout.

The process for making an elevation drawing is similar to creating a final design plan, as described in the last few pages.

TOOLS & MATERIALS

- Calculator
- Drafting pencil or pen
- Drafting triangle
- Ruler
- Tracing paper
- Colored pencils

Step A: Outline the Elevations

1. Convert the actual elevation measurements taken when you conducted the yard survey (page 96), to scale measurements (page 100). If practical, use a scale of ¼" = 1 ft. or ½" = 1 ft., which lets you show more detail than is possible in a ⅛" scale.
2. On a blank sheet of paper, draw a side view of each elevation site to scale.
3. Use sheets of tracing paper taped over the site drawings to test different design ideas. When planning a fence or deck, for example, make one sketch for each different style you're considering. Or, when planning the treatment for a steep slope, compare the effect of building one tall wall as opposed to several terraced walls over the course of the slope.

Step B: Complete the Elevation

1. Once you've selected the best design, carefully draft a final elevation drawing on fresh tracing paper, then photocopy it. Use colored pencils or pens to add color to all elements of the drawing.
2. Mark down all important height and length measurements on the elevation.
3. Draw a key, indicating compass directions and the scale at which the elevation is drawn.

A: *Draw an elevation view of each site to scale, using a ruler and drafting triangle. Test design ideas by overlaying sheets of tracing paper on the elevation drawing, and sketching variations.*

B: *For each elevation, select the best design variation and make a photocopy of this tracing. Use colored pencils to add color to all elements of the drawing. Note the important measurements of all components.*

Landscape Symbols

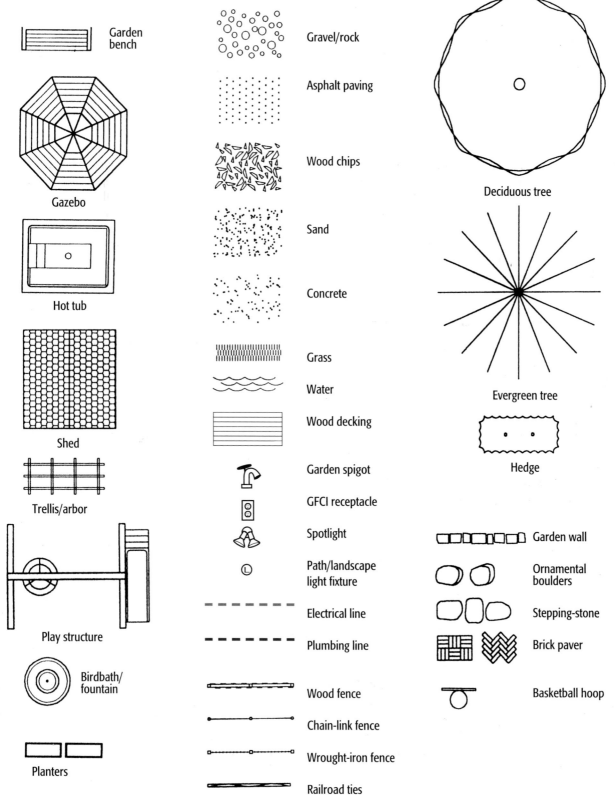

Garden bench

Gazebo

Hot tub

Shed

Trellis/arbor

Play structure

Birdbath/fountain

Planters

Gravel/rock

Asphalt paving

Wood chips

Sand

Concrete

Grass

Water

Wood decking

Garden spigot

GFCI receptacle

Spotlight

Path/landscape light fixture

Electrical line

Plumbing line

Wood fence

Chain-link fence

Wrought-iron fence

Railroad ties

Deciduous tree

Evergreen tree

Hedge

Garden wall

Ornamental boulders

Stepping-stone

Brick paver

Basketball hoop

Plans

Creating Working Plans

By now, you're probably getting eager to start work on your landscape, but there's one small step left to complete: drawing up working plans.

Working plans for a landscape serve the same function as blueprints did for the contractors who built your house. A working plan is a bare-bones version of a plan drawing or elevation that includes only the measurements and specifications needed to actually construct the landscape. The goal now is to create working plans that contain all the vital measurements and specifications.

Working plans help you estimate the amounts of materials you'll need and make it easier to schedule and organize the work. Or, if you plan to hire land-scape contractors or nursery professionals to work on your landscape, these plans will serve as the blue-print that guides their work.

Unless your landscape project is very simple, it's a good idea to create several working plans: a *demolition plan*, a *hardscape plan*, and one or more *planting maps*. If your project is very large, you may want to create a separate series of drawings for each of the different rooms in your outdoor home.

Step A: Create a Hardscape Plan

The hardscape plan includes the details of any major construction work your landscape will require.
1. Make a fresh tracing of your final design drawing (page 104) in pencil or black pen, featuring only the hardscape elements, such as paving, wood decking, fences, edgings, wiring, and plumbing lines. Make sure this drawing uses the same scale as your final design.
2. Use colored pencils to outline only the new hard-scape elements.
3. Add dimension lines and measurements to indi-cate the sizes of all the new hardscape features.
4. In the margins of the hardscape plan, write down any information that will be helpful when you shop and place orders for materials. For paved surfaces, for example, you can indicate square footage, thickness of paving materials, supplier, and price.
5. Where necessary, draw side-view elevations for any details that can't be included in the overhead hard-

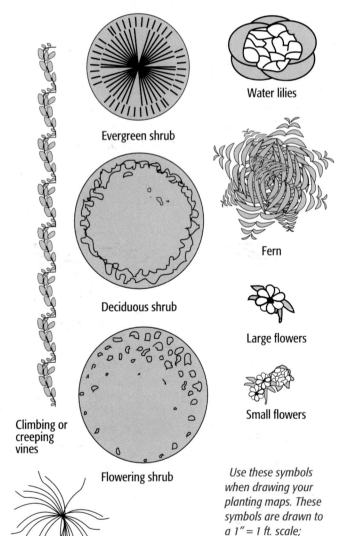

Evergreen shrub

Deciduous shrub

Climbing or creeping vines

Flowering shrub

Ornamental grass

Water lilies

Fern

Large flowers

Small flowers

Use these symbols when drawing your planting maps. These symbols are drawn to a 1" = 1 ft. scale; reduce them on a photocopier if you're using a smaller scale.

A: *Create a hardscape plan that gives all measurements and other specifications you'll need to order the materials and build your landscape.*

108

scape plan. On a sloped yard, for example, you may need an elevation to show the dimensions of terraces formed with retaining walls.

Step B: Create a Demolition Plan

The demolition plan will help you plan and schedule the major removal work, such as breaking up and removing old paving, cutting down trees, and stripping away grass.

1. Make a fresh tracing or photocopy of your site map (page 100), including all the current hard- and soft-scape features of your landscape.

2. In colored pencil or pen, highlight the elements that will be removed, demolished, or moved.

3. Note any information that is important for the demolition process. If trees need to be cut down, for example, indicate any obstacles, such as utility wires or neighboring buildings. If you'll be demolishing concrete or masonry, indicate how thick the slab is, and any rental tools that may be needed. If you'll be moving sod or other plants from one spot to another, indicate their destinations.

4. Create a step-by-step sequence and schedule for the demolition tasks, and mark this sequence on the margins of the plan.

Step C: Create a Planting Map

Draw a planting map for each ornamental planting area you plan to include in your new landscape. Creating a separate map for each area will let you use a large, easy-to-read scale. You don't need to include large trees and shrubs that are already shown in your other working plans.

1. Draw the outline of each decorative planting area on a sheet of paper. Using a large scale, such as 1" = 1 ft. will make it easy to see the detail in your planting map.

2. Using the symbols on the opposite page, mark the locations of all plants to be included.

3. Make notes indicating how many plants of each type you'll need. As you comparison shop, jot down the best sources for each plant type.

DESIGN TIP:

Design your planting areas so each ornamental species is repeated in groups of at least three plants. The same advice holds for shrubs and small trees. Groups of three or more look more natural than individual shrubs scattered around the yard.

And avoid using too many different species of flowers. When you begin gardening for the first time, it's tempting to use many different plants, but such a landscape usually looks fragmented and confused. It's better to stick with five or six attractive, easy-to-grow species and use them consistently throughout the yard.

B: *Create a demolition plan that highlights the hardscape and softscape elements you'll be removing before building your new landscape.*

C: *Create planting maps for each border garden and planting bed you'll be installing. Note the species and number of plants in the margins.*

Good-bye

We've had a great deal of fun sharing our views about landscaping with you. The writers, designers, gardeners, editors, artists, and photographers who contributed to this book all share a love of landscaping and the outdoors, which makes working long hours on such a project a great deal of fun. Saying farewell can be a bit sad, especially if you're leaving an enjoyable experience; but saying good-bye can also be exciting, particularly if the future holds great promise.

We hope you've enjoyed dreaming about your new outdoor home and making plans to create it. After reading this book, you have a new way of looking at landscaping and know many of the commonsense techniques and tips used by professional landscape designers.

More than anything else, we hope we've sparked your creativity, coaxed you into stretching your imagination, and given you confidence that designing a uniquely personal, functional outdoor home is well within your abilities. You're now in a great position to begin the next adventure—building your outdoor home.

We'd like to encourage you to drop us a letter or E-mail note if you have questions, comments, or ideas to share with us as you move from planning your landscape to building it. Your opinions will help guide our decisions regarding upcoming books on landscaping and gardening, and may help us plan future editions of this book. We'd like to hear about your experiences as you follow the design process outlined here, and we'd love to see photos of your finished landscape once it's built.

As you prepare to create your landscape, the logical next step will be for you to find some good books on landscape construction. Some of our favorite books are listed on the opposite page, but there are many other good publications, as well. Landscape magazines can also be a great source of information on outdoor construction. If you come across other books and publications you find especially helpful for designing and building landscapes, let us know so we can recommend them to others.

You can write to us at:

Outdoor Home Publications
Home Improvement Group
Creative Publishing international
5900 Green Oak Drive
Minnetonka, MN 55343

or, you can E-mail us at:

Btrandem@creativepub.com

Appendix

ADDITIONAL READING

Building Your Outdoor Home:
30 Easy Landscape Projects
Creative Publishing international
112 pages

Landscape Design & Construction
Creative Publishing international
128 pages

A Portfolio of Landscape Ideas
Creative Publishing international
96 pages

A Portfolio of Water Garden
& Specialty Landscape Ideas
Creative Publishing international
96 pages

A Portfolio of Fence & Gate Ideas
Creative Publishing international
96 pages

A Portfolio of Porch & Patio Ideas
Creative Publishing international
96 pages

The Garden Planner
by Robin Williams
Barron's
168 pages

Garden Design
by Robin Williams
Reader's Digest
208 pages

The Principles of Gardening
by Hugh Johnson
Fireside
272 pages

Landscaping from the Ground Up
by Sara Jane von Trapp
Taunton Books
168 pages

The Complete Home
Landscape Designer
by Joel Lerner
St. Martin's Press
118 pages

Backyard Design
by Jean Spiro Breskend
Bulfinch
224 pages

The Outdoor Room
by David Stevens
Random House
192 pages

The Natural Garden
by Ken Druse
Crown Publishing Group
296 pages

USEFUL ADDRESSES
The following groups may have helpful information if you're looking for a good landscape professional

American Society of
Landscape Architects
1733 Connecticut Ave. NW
Washington, DC 20009

American Horticultural Society
7931 East Boulevard Drive
Alexandria, VA 22308

WEB SITES
Garden.com

Gardening.com

Fine Gardening Magazine
www.taunton.com/fg/

PHOTO CREDITS
Photographers:

©Walter Chandoha:
pages 2a, 32, 35a, 67, 74

©Crandall & Crandall/Nick
Williams & Associates: page 13b

©Crandall & Crandall:
pages 15b, 81a

©Crandall & Crandall/Michael
Glassman & Associates: page 62b

©Crandall & Crandall/Greg
Grisamore & Associates: page 66a

©R. Todd Davis: page 65a

©Derek Fell: pages 16, 25a, 75b,
83c, 99

©Saxon Holt: pages 11b, 22, 65b, 75a

©Mark A. Madsen: page 9

©Charles Mann: pages 11a, 34c,
39b, 66b, 68, 72, 77

©Karen Melvin/Kay Thalhuber
Design Group: page 5

©Karen Melvin/Judy Onofrio:
page 21a

©Karen Melvin/Sylvestre
Construction: page 37b

©Karen Melvin: pages 79, 81c, 83b

©Karen Melvin/Mike McGuire
Architect: page 83a

©Jerry Pavia: pages 21b, 34a,
64a, 69c, 73b

©Robert Perron: page 81b

Manufacturers:

Anderson Design Services, Ltd.:
pages 31b, 54, 57, 71, 73a

Bachman's Landscaping Service:
pages 17b, 30a, 33b, 33d, 39a

By the Yard, Inc.: page 49a

California Redwood Association:
pages 13a, 43a, 62a

Featherock, Inc.: page 37c

Hunter Industries: page 36a

Idaho Wood Lighting: page 36b

Interlock Concrete Products, Inc.:
page 31a

Intermatic Inc.: page 37d

Lifetime, Inc.: page 19b

Lloyd®/Flanders All-Weather
Wicker: cover, 38a

Milt Charno & Associates, Inc.:
page 31c

TCT Landscaping: page 23a

Weatherend Estate Furniture:
pages 3a, 25b

Weber-Stephen Products Co.:
page 37a

Index

A
Accents, 39, 65
Air-conditioning unit, 27
Annuals, 52-53
Arbors, 34-35
Architectural harmony, 74
Archways, 11, 17, 34
Ashlars, 45
Asphalt, 19, 31
Awnings, 13, 15, 23, 35

B
Backstop, 15
Badminton, 19
Balance, 68-69
Balled-and-burlapped plants, 57
Balusters, 42
Barbecue, 11, 13, 37
Bare-root plants, 57
Bark, 30-31, 42-43
Basics, 6-57
Benches, 11, 17, 19, 21, 23, 25, 38, 42
Berms, 33
Birdbaths, 11, 39
Border gardens, 33
Brainstorming, 88-89
Bricks, 19, 23, 25, 46, 64
    paver, 13, 17, 31, 46
Bubble plans, sketching, 102-103
Budgeting, 90-91
Building Codes, 19, 92-95
Bulbs, 54

C
Cedar, 42
Ceilings, 35
Chain-link fences, 15, 17, 19, 27, 48
Chairs, 23, 25, 38, 43
Cobblestone, 31, 45
Codes, courtesies and, 92-95
Color harmony, 74-75
Color scheme, 65, 69
Compost heap, 27
Concrete, 17, 19, 23, 31, 46-47
Connectors, 48
Container plants, 57
Cost, 40, 65
Croquet, 19, 23

D
Deciduous trees, 57
Decks, 13, 23, 31, 35, 42
    legal restrictions, 95
Decorative blocks, 46
Decorative movement, 71
Design concepts, 60-75
Design, drafting a final, 104-105
Dining areas, 12-13
Doors and windows, 13, 34
Drinking fountain, 15, 19, 36
Driveways, 17, 31, 47, 93

E
Edging materials, 31, 46, 49
Electrical outlets, 13, 36
Elements, 28-39

Elevations, drawing, 106
Emotional interest, 73
Entry lighting, 11
Evergreens, 57

F
Fabric, landscape, 49
Fences, 15, 19, 25, 27, 32, 42, 48-49
Final design, 104-105
Fire pit, 12, 15, 23, 25, 37
Fireplace, 13, 37
Fitness and sports, 18-19
Fixtures and utilities, 36-37
Flagstones, 17, 31, 45
Floodlights, 36
Flooring boards, 42
Floors, 30-31
Flower garden beds, 11, 39
    legal restrictions, 94
Fountains, 11, 25, 36-37, 39
Foyer, 10-11
Front rooms, 10-11
Furnishings, 38-39, 65

G
Gardening, 21
Garden sheds, 26-27
Garden walls, 32-33
Gas cooktop, 37
Gates, 11, 15, 17, 34, 43
Gazebo, 23, 25, 35
Grass, *see*: Lawn, grass
Gravel, 44-45
    smooth pea, 15, 19, 30-31, 45
Ground cover, 30, 56

H
Hardscape materials, 40, 65, 69
Harmony, 74-75
Hedges, 32-33
Hobby spaces, 20-21
Hot tubs, 37

I
Information, gathering, 86-97
Interest, 72-73

K
Kids, spaces for, 14-15

L
Landscape lighting, 11, 17, 21, 25, 36
Landscape style, 76-83
Landscape symbols, 107
Lawn, grass, 11, 16-17, 19, 23, 25, 30, 56
Lighting, 11, 13, 15, 17, 19, 21, 23, 25, 36-37
    legal restrictions, 94
Loose-fill materials, 17, 25, 30-31
Lumber, plastic, 49

M
Maintenance, 65
Making plans, 84-109
Maps, creating site, 100-101
Masonry, 13, 34, 46
Materials, 40-49
Metals, 48
Movement, 70-71

P
Passageways, 16-17
Pathways, 31
    legal restrictions, 93

Patios, 11, 13, 23, 31
    legal restrictions, 94
Paved courtyard, 11
Perennials, 54-55
Pergolas, 34-35, 42
Pet spaces, 27
Plans, 98-109
Planters, 23
Planting areas, 11
    raised beds, 15, 21
Plants, 50-57
Plastics and metals, 48-49
Ponds, 25
Principles, 58-83
Private retreats, 24-25
Pruning, 57
Purpose, 62-63

R
Recreation areas, 22-23
Roofs, 13, 15
Rooms, 8-27

S
Safety, 11, 15, 17
Sand, 15, 19
Seats, 19
Shrubs and trees, 11, 57
Sidewalks, 17
Simplicity, 64-65
Sinks, 13
Site map, creating, 100-101
Sound systems, 23
Sports and fitness, 18-19
Sprinkler, underground, 11, 21
Stairs, 17
Statues, 11, 17, 25
Stepping-stone pathways, 17
Stone and soil, 23, 44-45
    manufactured stone, 46-47
    natural stone, 13, 17, 25
Styles, catalog of traditional, 78-83
Swimming pools, 18-19, 23
Swings, 15

T
Tables, 23, 25
Traditional styles, catalog of, 78-83
Trellises, 13, 25
Trees and shrubs, 57

U
Unity, 66-67
Utilities and fixtures, 36-37
Utility spaces, 26-27

V
Vegetable gardens, 13
Visual arts, 21
Volleyball, 19

W
Walkways, 17
Walls, 32-33
Wildlife study, 20-21
Windows and doors, 13, 34
Wood, 23, 42-43
Working plans, creating, 108-109

Y
Yard survey, 96-97